I0450287

1st DORSAL FIN

GILL OPENINGS

SPIRACLE

EYE

NOSTRIL

MOUTH

AXIL

PECTORAL FIN

INNER CORNER

PELVIC FIN

ANAL FIN

2nd DORSAL FIN

CAUDAL PEDUNCLE

CAUDAL FIN

Secret World Of
The Sharks

Secret World Of

THE SHARKS

Robert F. Burgess

AN AUTHORS GUILD BACKINPRINT.COM EDITION

Secret World Of
The Sharks

AN AUTHORS GUILD BACKINPRINT.COM EDITION

Published by iUniverse.com, Inc.

For information address:
iUniverse.com, Inc.
620 North 48th Street, Suite 201
Lincoln, NE 68504-3467
www.iuniverse.com

Originally published by Doubleday

Author photo by Charles Harnage Jr.

ISBN: 0-595-09499-6

Printed in the United States of America

This book is dedicated to
DR. JIM THOMPSON
my friend and companion
of many adventures afield and afloat

ACKNOWLEDGMENTS

A book of this kind could not have been written without the help and cooperation of many individuals. I would like to take this opportunity to express my gratitude to those who so kindly shared their knowledge, their time and their efforts with me in making it possible.

I am particularly indebted to the scientists and technicians of the Mote Marine Laboratory at Sarasota, Florida, for the invaluable assistance they gave me while I was there. It is with special appreciation that I thank biochemist Captain H. David Baldridge, Jr, USN, and Dr. Perry W. Gilbert, Executive Director of the Laboratory and Chairman of the AIBS Shark Research Panel. Dr. Gilbert and Captain Baldridge not only took time out of their busy schedules to demonstrate various research procedures and to make themselves available for lengthy interviews, but they also patiently read the scientific portions of this manuscript. Their criticisms and suggestions were of immeasurable value in clarifying and amplifying these chapters. In addition, I would like to express my appreciation to Captain Hugh H. Scott and his wife, Roberta, for their many kindnesses, including their efforts to help me obtain photographs of the capture, retrieving and dissecting of twelve large brown sharks.

I am also indebted to fishery biologist Stewart Springer of the U. S. Fish and Wildlife Service for permission to use the excellent shark species illustrations which he generously made available to me. Others who have contributed materially to the preparation of this work are: research biologist John G. Casey, Bureau of Sport Fisheries and Wildlife; Dan Saults, Chief, Office of Conservation Education, Bureau of Sport Fisheries and Wildlife; John A. Guinan, Information Officer, Bureau of Commercial Fisheries; Andrew H. Planey, Public Information Officer, Naval Ship Research and Development Laboratory, Panama City, Florida, and David W. Redman, Assistant Director of Public Relations, Marineland of Florida.

I would also like to thank a number of very close friends who have made my task easier in many ways. They include my "personal" librarian, Miss Marjorie Barnes, who can always be counted on to locate the unlocatable research items for me; my ingenious and always cooperative shark-fishing friend of Boynton Beach Inlet, Herb Goodman; and last but not least, my fifty fellow anglers of the Florida Shark Club of Jacksonville without whose initial inspiration this book might never have been written.

Contents

1 Shark Myths, Men and Gods   13

2 Shark Attack!   24

3 Sharks Out of the Past   35

4 Anatomy of a Shark   41

5 The Man-eaters   56

6 Fighting the Menace   76

7 Shark Fishing   87

8 The Shark Specialists   99

9 Schoolmistress of Sharks   111

10 Porpoises vs. Sharks   119

11 Science and Sharks   126

12 Barbarian or Benefactor?   138

CONTENTS

APPENDIX I *How to Identify a Shark*   142

APPENDIX II *U. S. Navy "Shark Danger"
                 Ratings*   149

APPENDIX III *Maximum Sizes of Common
                   Species of Sharks*   150

BIBLIOGRAPHY   151
INDEX   154

The Sharks

1

Shark Myths, Men and Gods

Imagine yourself standing on the fine white sand beach of a coral atoll in the South Pacific. Behind you is the soft whisper of rustling palms, the faint fragrance of wild frangipani. Before you is a lagoon, glimmering and cool like a turquoise mirror enclosed in an oval frame. The invitation is too great to resist. Into the water you go, suddenly free of all weight, all awkwardness, as your flippered feet propel you swiftly through the subsurface of liquid blue space. Sound ceases except for the measured rumble of air escaping from your scuba regulator. Through the tunnel vision of your face mask, the pass appears—a yawning dark green gate that breaches the misty rim of white rock and opens into the depths beyond.

You dive, spiraling downward through a rainbow of fish of all sizes and shapes, your ears pinging as you clear them under the increasing pressures . . . down toward the broken coral heads, the fragmented brown elkhorns, towering sea whips, golden-fanned gorgonians. And then you pause over an ivory tongue of sand to marvel at the startling kaleidoscopic beauty of the reef. You see the gently swaying sea fans, feel the cool surge sweeping in from the pass, hear the constant clicking of the shrimp. You are at peace with the world—when suddenly everything changes.

An abrupt hush falls over the reef. Where an instant before there were a myriad shifting shoals of colorful fish, all have vanished. Even the coral's bright hues seem to fade as if a cloud has passed over the sun. Then, beyond the misty green break in the reef wall, a dim shape appears, grows big, looms even larger, until it fills the opening and sweeps through in a long gray shape, its pointed snout surrounded by striped pilot fish, its ugly underslung mouth bristling with crooked teeth. There seems to be no end to the huge streamlined body that glides in with its wide pectorals rigid as wings, its barreled white belly bearded with remora. As the monster sweeps past, its glittering round eye fixes you with a cold, menacing stare. It circles once, twice, and then, with a flick of its broad caudal fin, the lord of the reef swerves back through the pass and disappears in the distant green gloom from which it came.

What you have seen is the indisputable sovereign of the seas— the shark. Hammerhead, thresher, great white, mako, blacktip, tiger or blue whaler, no matter what name man has given him, he is a fearsome brute, an almost perfect engine of destruction with finely balanced instincts of curiosity and caution. He comes out of the remote corridors of time virtually unchanged, a primitive creature that can be traced back in a direct line over 180 million years. Since man's earliest beginnings he has been in conflict with this ageless enemy— one of the most puzzling species in the sea.

Seafaring men of the past knew him as the ominous shadow that pursued their sailing vessels for days on end, appearing and disappearing in the foaming wakes—always alert, always eager to gulp down anything that fell or was thrown overboard. It was the shark who was the supreme diabolical villain of almost every seafaring yarn ever spun. He was the possessor of the ominous sickle-shaped fin that sliced across the still surfaces of tropical lagoons to strike panic in the heart of all who saw it. He was the crescent-mouthed terror of the deep that attacked pearl divers without warning, his jagged teeth often "biting them in twain." He was the creature about which so little was known that in the early days of voyage and discovery there was not even an English word for him. He was known only by the Spanish name *tiburon*.

In 1555 Eden wrote in his *Descades:* "The tiburon is a very great fysshe and very quicke and swifte in the water and a cruell devourer." In 1497, when Antonio Pigafetta accompanied Vasco da Gama on his trip around Africa, he wrote about the tiburons they saw at Sierra Leones, "which have teeth of a terrible kind and eat people when they find them in the sea either dead or alive." In a letter written from Cochin, China, in 1580, a sea traveler described a fatal attack by a shark:

"I have seen many great fish. . . . What called forth still greater surprise on my part were other big fishes, that are in the ocean and that eat man alive, whereof I have been myself a witness. For when a man fell from our ship into the sea during a strong wind, so that we could not wait for him or come to his rescue in any other fashion, we threw out to him on a rope a wooden block, especially prepared for that purpose, and this he finally managed to grasp and thought he could save himself thereby.

"But when our crew drew this block with the man toward the ship and had him within half the carrying distance of a musket shot, there appeared from below the surface of the sea a large monster called Tiburon, it rushed on the man and tore him to pieces before our very eyes."

Other lurid tales concerning the rapacious man-eating tendencies of these sea monsters drifted back from sixteenth-century voyages to India, Africa and the Pacific. It is uncertain how or when the word "shark" replaced "tiburon" in the English language, but some scholars believe that it derived from the German word *Schurke*, meaning "villain." At any rate, the word "shark" appears to have come into use around 1569 when sailors of the Sir John Hopkins' fleet returned from a freebooting expedition against the Spanish and brought home a shark that was put on exhibit in London.

One of the earliest pictorial records of a shark attack was discovered on the fragments of a vase excavated at Lacco Ameno, Ischia. The design depicts shipwrecked sailors, one of whom is being devoured by a man-eating fish. The vase is believed to have been made about 725 B.C.

Early historians obviously lacked much information about sharks, which is not surprising since contemporary man is only now beginning to understand them. And oddly enough, the Egyptians, for all their great knowledge, failed to acknowledge the shark. In their many writings and paintings of animals, birds and reptiles, the shark is absent. Nor is he mentioned in the Bible. The ancient Greek word *kētos* and the Hebrew word *tānnin* were used by early historians to denote any large marine animal. In the Bible these words have been translated as "great fish" or "dragon." In light of our present knowledge about whales, there is doubt that Jonah was ever swallowed by a whale as is popularly believed. Whales are mammals and sharks are fish. Although the ancients could not be expected to know the biological difference, some believe it is more likely that the "great fish" in the Bible that swallowed and regurgitated Jonah was a harmless, plankton-eating whale shark, the largest fish in the sea. As early as the middle 1700s, Linnaeus, the famed Swedish naturalist, said that he believed the fish responsible for this miraculous feat was the great white shark. If he were correct, it would indeed be a miracle, for the great white shark seldom releases his victims intact.

The Greeks were perhaps the first people to focus more than casual attention upon sharks. The earliest known writings about them are found in ancient Greek legends. The historian Herodotus described shark attacks upon shipwrecked sailors of the Persian fleet in 492 B.C. About 150 years later, the Greek philosopher Aristotle knew enough about sharks to be able to write in detail on the differences

Portrait of a killer—the Great White or Man-eater shark, unquestionably the most dangerous species known to man.

between several species. Pliny (A.D. 23–79) described the perilous battles between sponge divers and sharks; while the Greek poet Leonidas of Tarentum wrote a graphic account of a sailor who was bitten in two by a sea monster. Since his companions buried his remains on the beach, the man was therefore buried, according to the poet, "both on land and in the sea."

Throughout history the shark has been the antithesis of evil, inflated to monstrous proportions by legends and myths. Most of these stories originated in the South Pacific, where the shark was both feared and worshiped as a supernatural god. These fables have all the qualities of our fairy tales, with this difference: in one form or another, the evil character possessing the magical powers is always a shark. In his book *Shark! Shark!*, a classic account of the early days of commercial shark fishing, Captain William E. Young relates the legend told most often by the old Kanakas of Hawaii. It concerns Kamo-hoa-lii, the king of all sharks that frequent Hawaiian waters.

According to the ancient storyteller, Kamo-hoa-lii, the shark god, lived in deep underwater caverns on the island of Hawaii. Usually he spent most of his time swimming in the ocean, but occasionally he liked to swim through an inlet into a secluded pool surrounded by steep cliffs in the beautiful Waipo Valley. One day while Kamo-hoa-lii was enjoying a swim in the pool he saw a beautiful girl named Kalei, who had come there to gather shellfish. Kalei was slender and graceful, a good diver and an excellent swimmer. She was prettier than any girl the shark god had ever seen, and he immediately fell in love with her.

But Kalei seldom came to the pool alone; she was always accompanied by other girls. So Kamo-hoa-lii began visiting the pool more often, swimming back and forth in its azure depths in the hope of glimpsing Kalei and perhaps discovering some way to meet her. One day when the sea was very rough and the other girls were afraid to go after shellfish, Kalei came to the pool alone. As soon as Kamo-hoa-lii saw her he realized that this was the opportunity he had been waiting for.

But the shark god knew he could not afford to let the girl see him in his present form, for fear of frightening her. So, calling upon all his magical powers, he transformed himself into a handsome man who swam ashore and struck up an acquaintance with the lovely girl. Although Kalei tried not to show it, she was as attracted to the charming young man as he was to her. Their friendship ripened into love and the following spring she became his wife. Shortly before their first child was born, Kamo-hoa-lii told Kalei that he had to leave, but before going he explained to her who he really was and left explicit instructions on how she should rear the child. Most important of all, he warned, the youngster must never be fed animal flesh of any kind.

Kalei gave birth to a strong, healthy boy who appeared to be as normal as any other child, except that on his back, between his shoulder blades, he had the mouth of a shark. Kalei told no one about this except her family, taking care that others did not find out by seeing to it that the boy always wore a fine *kapa* cloak over his shoulders and back. She named the boy Nanaue and warned the family about feeding him meat. But when Nanaue became old enough to fall under the taboo requiring the men to eat alone, his grandfather forgot, and fed him his first taste of pork, believing that all boys must have meat if they were to grow into strong, courageous men. Once Nanaue ate meat he took every opportunity he could find to taste more. He also found that now when he swam by himself in the pool near his home he was able to turn himself into a shark and speedily catch the fish that tried to avoid him.

As Nanaue matured into a man his appetite for meat grew more intense. By now he was also the subject of much local gossip. The villagers wondered why he kept to himself so much, and especially why the handsome, athletic young man always wore a cloak over his back. Nanaue knew about the gossip but he paid no attention to it. He was content to work in his mother's potato patch, which afforded him a fine view of the path leading down to the pool where he and the other villagers swam. Frequently, whenever people passed on their way to the beach, Nanaue called a cheerful greeting and warned them to be careful while they were swimming. For it was well known in the village that from time to time people who visited the pool alone never returned. But what no one else knew was that Nanaue often followed the solitary swimmers to the pool. Then, in the form of a shark, he attacked and made a meal of them.

No one would have suspected what the shark-man was doing had it not been for the king ordering all able-bodied young men on the island to join a work gang that was to farm one of the royal plantations. While Nanaue was working on the plantation the other men began kidding him about the cape he wore. What began as good-natured teasing turned into something far more serious when two of the men jerked off the cape and revealed the snapping jaws of the shark's mouth on Nanaue's back.

At first they were shocked, then horrified, as they realized that he was a shark-man. In the ensuing struggle to restrain him, several men were bitten, but Nanaue managed to escape. The news quickly spread across the island. Now people knew what had caused the strange disappearances. When the king learned about Nanaue he ordered him caught and cast into a great fire. But just as the villagers were closing in on him, Nanaue leaped into the sea, where he immediately changed into a huge shark and swam away from the island of Hawaii forever.

His next stop was the island of Maui, where he went ashore in the shape of a man and befriended the people, who thought he was a traveler from Hawaii. In time he married the chief's daughter, but soon he slipped into his old habits. One by one people began disappearing as they had on Hawaii, and finally Nanaue was caught in the act by two fishermen who saw him push a girl into the water, then leap in to devour her as a shark. Realizing that he had been discovered, Nanaue swam off toward the island of Molokai.

Once again the people accepted the handsome young stranger in their midst, and it was only a matter of time before the shark-man took advantage of their hospitality by pursuing lone bathers and seeing to it that they never returned. The disappearances became so frequent on Molokai that the frightened people finally consulted a shark priest. After much prayerful meditation the kahuna told them to seize Nanaue and pull off his cape and there they would find the answer to their troubles.

That evening seven warriors ambushed Nanaue as he was following a girl to the beach. They tore off his cape and saw at once that he was the dreaded shark-man. Without delay they bound him and sent word to the villagers to build a huge fire in the hills so that the curse of their island could be destroyed.

But as Nanaue lay on the beach straining against his bonds he knew that if he could simply roll into the water he could effect the transformation that might save his life. He struggled and strained and finally managed to get close enough for the waves to lap over his body. Immediately he changed into a wildly thrashing shark.

When the villagers saw what was happening they leaped forward with ropes and nets until the floundering shark was so well enmeshed that he could never escape.

Then, laboriously, all the people joined in hauling the bound sea monster up the slopes to the waiting fire built of bamboo taken from the sacred grove of Kain-alu hill, where Nanaue, the shark-man, finally met his end. The great groove caused by the passage of his body up that hill can be seen to this day, and the place ever afterward has been known as Puumano, Shark Hill.

It is also said that the god Mohoalii was so angered by the desecration of the sacred bamboo of Kain-alu, which had always made the hardest, keenest knives, that he took away the sharpness and hardness of this cane grove forever. This is why the bamboo on Shark Hill at Molokai has always been softer and weaker than any other throughout the islands.

During the early nineteenth century shark worship was common among the South Sea Islanders. Various species of sharks were deified. Temples were erected. Shark priests and the natives prayed and made offerings to appease their various shark gods. While one tribe of islanders worshiped a certain species of shark, those of a neighboring island often worshiped another. Inter-island wars frequently broke out when it was learned that the natives of one island killed the sacred sharks worshiped by another.

When the United States Navy dredged up the bottom of the harbor to install a $4 million drydock during the construction of a major sea base at Pearl Harbor, they destroyed the remnants of an ancient shark pen. This pen was originally a circular enclosure of lava rock that covered a four-acre area on the beach. In olden times it was used for shark worship and gladiatorial events that must have rivaled those of ancient Rome.

One end of the pen opened onto the sea. Sharks were enticed into this enclosure with fish and human bait, then the sea wall was closed and the sharks slowly starved for the festive events that were to take place. According to ancient Hawaiian legends these rituals were put on for the amusement of the Queen Shark, who watched from her regal lair at the bottom of the harbor. They consisted of duels between the sharks and Hawaiian gladiators who entered the pen to fight until death claimed one or the other of the combatants.

Early seamen enjoyed the excitement of shark fishing. In the days of sail, sharks often followed vessels and fed on refuse thrown overboard. From an old print.

The warriors were armed only with a primitive shark dagger consisting of a short broomstick-thick piece of wood with a single shark tooth imbedded on the side of it. When clenched in the fist, the tooth protruded between two of the warrior's fingers. Unlike many duels between man and beast where a mistake might give the man at least a second chance, these were one-time, life-or-death encounters. The warrior would let the shark attack him, then at the last instant he had to avoid the snapping jaws, dive beneath the hurtling body and try to rip open the shark's belly with his crude weapon. It is unlikely that many warriors survived the unequal duel, but Hawaiian legend says that some did.

When the foundations of the Pearl Harbor drydock built over the ancient shark pen suddenly collapsed from an underwater eruption, old residents had their own explanation for the disaster. "Queen Shark is angry and humps her back," they said.

Man has co-existed with sharks for the last two thousand years, yet he has learned surprisingly little about them. This lack of knowledge has created myths that are still believed by many people today. One of the reasons for this is that writers of the past who supposedly were reporting accurately about sharks frequently relied more on their imaginations than on facts. The author of a natural history book published in 1889 had these words of wisdom to impart regarding the nature and function of shark teeth. "[The shark's] large and cavernous mouth is located beneath the snout and is armed with six rows above and four rows below, of bristling, compressed and sharp pointed teeth, *which are moveable at the creature's will.*" After this inaccuracy the author compounds the error by letting his imagination elaborate. "When the animal is disturbed, these teeth lay flat upon the palate directed backward; or, in other words, [they] remain shut up like a jack-knife; but at the moment he pounces upon his prey they are erected, filling the mouth with weapons that are the very inspiration of terror." From here on he gives his imagination free rein. "A singular power is exhibited in the shark in his ability to erect one or more rows of teeth at a time as occasionally required; thus if he attacks a puny prey only the front row of teeth is used, while a larger may call for two rows, and for a strong or fierce antagonist his mouth is made to bristle with teeth from which nothing once caught can possibly escape."

In the twentieth century many people still believe in the myths that a shark must roll over on its back to seize its prey; that its eyesight is poor; and—most popular of all—that a shark will not attack a person in shallow water. From time to time the public is exposed to debunking articles in the popular magazines. These come in cycles. One year the stories stress the deadliness of sharks; the next year sharks are downgraded and some other marine species such as barracuda are blamed for the annual deaths and mutilations of bathers. These stories do nothing but confuse the public and obscure the truth.

In 1959 there were thirty-six unprovoked shark attacks upon man. These tragedies marked the year the myths began to die.

2

Shark Attack!

At five o' clock on May 7, 1959, it was a sunny afternoon at Baker's Beach on San Francisco Bay. The water was cool, but it looked deliciously inviting to eighteen-year-old Albert Kogler and Shirley O'Neill, who had come to the beach to go swimming. It was a perfect spring day without a cloud in the sky, and they could not resist stretching out in the sun for a few minutes before going into the water. Finally, the sparkling blue bay beckoned. Gritting their teeth and cheerfully braving the chilly water, they splashed in and started swimming. What happened after that was to shock readers around the world. Shirley O'Neill's graphic statement to the press reveals what occurred.

"We'd been in for about fifteen minutes and were out maybe forty or fifty yards, when he said:

" 'We're out pretty far now, let's go no farther, it'd be too dangerous.' "

"We were treading water as we were talking. We were just about to start back and I was looking away from him toward the Golden Gate [to the east], when I heard him scream.

"I turned around and saw this big thing flap up into the air. I didn't know whether it was a fin or a tail. I knew it was some kind of fish.

"There was a thrashing in the water and I knew he was struggling with it. It must have been pretty big.

"He shouted, 'It's a shark . . . get out of here!'

"I started swimming back. I swam a few strokes, but I thought to myself, I just can't leave him here.

"I was scared and I didn't know what to do, but I knew I couldn't leave him.

"I turned around and took a couple of strokes back.

"He kept screaming. I could tell the fish was chewing him up. It was a horrible scream.

"All I could see was blood all over the water.

"He was shouting, 'Help me! Help me!'"

Summoning phenomenal courage, Shirley O'Neill swam back to Albert. Finding his left arm nearly bitten through at the shoulder, she put her arm around him and struggled for twenty minutes to get him almost ashore. There a fisherman threw her a line and pulled them the rest of the way.

On the beach Shirley prayed over the boy, but three hours later Albert Kogler died of his injuries. Tooth marks identified the killer as *Carcharodon caracharias*, the great white shark, the one to which the term man-eater is usually applied.

Five weeks later, on the afternoon of June 14, 1959, Gerald Lehrer and Robert L. Pamparin, a thirty-three-year-old Convair engineer, decided to dive for abalones at La Jolla Cove, a short distance north of San Diego. It was a bright sunny day and there were scores of bathers at the nearby popular swimming beach. But Lehrer and Pamparin had the coveted shellfish on their minds so they wasted no time donning face masks and fins and getting into the water. Pamparin was wearing blue fins, a pink bathing suit, black face mask and a pair of white gloves. Both divers were armed with yellow-handled abalone irons used to pry the mother-of-pearl shellfish off the bottom.

Pushing an inflated black innertube ahead of them, they quickly swam out to a spot fifty yards from a rocky point. There they up-ended and dove down to explore the bottom. Lehrer, a less experienced diver, worked closer to shore. After a brief trip underwater he came up. As he looked back toward his friend a short distance away, he suddenly saw a large dorsal fin slicing the surface toward Pamparin. He shouted a warning and pointed. Pamparin's body rose out of the water as if he had stepped up on a rock. He thrashed the water violently with his arms. His face mask was missing. Even as Lehrer swam toward him, Pamparin was dragged beneath the surface.

When Lehrer reached the spot he ducked his face underwater and looked through his mask. What he saw was a scene of horror. Pamparin was several feet below him staring straight up. The upper half of his body protruded from the jaws of a shark almost twenty feet long. A great wave of red discolored the water. Lehrer dove and made a futile attempt to frighten the shark into releasing Pamparin. When this failed he surfaced, shouted a warning to the other swimmers in the cove and swam ashore.

News of the attack spread swiftly. Life guards in boats and a Coast Guard helicopter started an immediate search. No trace of Pamparin was ever found, although the helicopter sighted one of his blue swim fins floating in the water some distance away. After sifting all the evidence, authorities concluded that Pamparin's killer was probably a great white shark.

During the fateful year of 1959, California was the scene of three more attacks. A month after Pamparin disappeared, twenty-five year-old Verne S. Fleet was attacked in the same general area between Alligator Head and Bloomer Beach near La Jolla. On July 28, Fleet was two hundred feet from shore, skindiving in clear water thirty feet deep. He was wearing a black rubber wet suit that covered his head, torso and arms, but left his legs bare. Diving to the bottom, he shot a small fish and tied it to his waist. As he rose to the surface to reload his speargun a three- to six-foot hammerhead shark attacked him and left fifteen tooth marks in his left thigh.

On October 4, at Bodega Bay, California, thirty-year-old James Hay was twenty feet below the surface hunting abalones with a companion. He swam to the surface but was suddenly dragged under by a violent jerk. A large white shark had grabbed his swim fin and was shaking him. Hay managed to escape with only his swim fin bitten.

Then on November 10, near Paradise Cove, Malibu, California, twenty-one-year-old Duffie Fryling was swimming through a school of two and a half- to five-foot sharks when he was attacked on the arm. The species of shark was unidentified.

Across the country that year, Florida was also experiencing its share of shark attacks. The first occurred on March 29 near Marathon, Florida. Between 1 and 2 P.M. that day thirteen-year-old James Mc-

The author poses with a large hammerhead caught during a club Sharkathon on the Florida east coast. The shark's eyes and nostrils are located on the ends of its unusual head lobes. This species has been involved in attacks against man.

Kee was swimming with three other boys in murky water when he was attacked. The shark bumped him, then bit him on the knee. The species was never identified.

Two months later, on May 3, just four days before the Kogler tragedy in California, an unusual attack took place near Panama City on northwest Florida's Gulf Coast. On that cloudy Sunday morning twenty-two-year-old Ernest Grover and his seventeen-year-old brother, Danny, set out with a group of friends in a boat to spearfish for cobia—a large migratory species of fish which when seen from a distance vaguely resembles a shark. Grover, like all the others in the group—Sonny McKiver, Ronnie Groom and Bradley Pitts, was a member of the Dolphin Skindiving Club of Panama City. All were experienced divers who had a healthy respect for the hazards the sea reserved for the careless or unwary.

A half mile offshore the group started diving. Visibility was poor, but as Grover's eyes became accustomed to the half gloom underwater he could distinguish the dim white sand bottom that stretched off into a milky blue haze in all directions. The water was cool and Grover was wearing a black rubber wet suit. After an hour of diving he exhausted the air supply of his scuba gear and left the heavy equipment in the boat with his brother, Danny, who did not dive. After that he finned along the surface, searching the depths.

It was about 10:30 when he saw his first fish below him. The cobia's long black shape resembled a cross between a giant catfish and a shark. Raising his head out of water, Grover yelled jokingly to McKiver some distance away. "Hey, Sonny! There's a shark circling below us!" Then, without waiting for a reply, he sucked in his breath and dove.

The cobia was moving slowly along the bottom. Not wishing to frighten the fish, Grover made his approach carefully, then lifted his speargun and fired.

The steel shaft thudded into the fish's side. The cobia reacted instantly, darting forward so suddenly that it almost wrenched the speargun out of Grover's hands. The fish made two more violent lunges and the spear pulled loose.

Grover surfaced, quickly hauled in the spear on its cable and recocked his speargun. Then he looked down to see if he could find the wounded fish.

The cobia was swimming some distance away, a thin trail of blood seeping from the wound in its side. Grover swam across the surface until he was over the quarry again. As he was about to flip over and go after it, another cobia swam into view. Fully aware that the wounded fish would be more wary this time, Grover decided to attack the newcomer.

Several swift kicks of his flippers sent him gliding down into spearing range of the second cobia. Once again he raised the gun, sighted and fired. The spear hit its mark, but again the powerful fish tore free. As Grover rose to the surface he glimpsed both fish circling him and trailing blood.

The moment he broke water he doubled up to recock his speargun. At that instant something slammed into him with such force that, as he recalled later, "I thought a boat had struck me!" Seconds later he knew it was a large shark.

From their boat seventy-five feet away the other skindivers stared in horror. Grover yelled for help. Danny tried desperately to start the motor and go to his brother's aid. "It was terrible," he said. "Water was splashing ten feet high. I couldn't start the motor and Ernie was hollering for help."

The shark had grabbed Grover's doubled-up body in its jaws and dragged him underwater. He knew that if he couldn't free himself the shark would shake him to pieces. He jabbed at the shark with his spear, but it wouldn't penetrate the tough hide. Then he did the only thing left to do—he rammed his hands and arms down into the shark's maw and tried to pry himself loose.

No one will ever be certain how or why it occurred, but the shark released Grover. Once free, he kicked as hard as he could with his one good leg and made it to another fishing boat that was closer to him than his brother's.

"I prayed that those two fishermen would pull in my legs before the shark came back around," said Grover.

They did. They were *Panama City News-Herald* fishing columnist Jim Sullivan and insurance salesman George Kimmel, who had been trolling nearby when Grover was attacked.

"It was very sudden," said Sullivan. "When we first saw the churning in the water we thought Grover had tangled a cobia in his harpoon line and was snarled in it. He hollered for help and then the churning stopped. He swam to our boat and we carried him ashore."

From the beach Grover was rushed to a hospital where doctors worked two and a half hours and took over seventy stitches to close wounds in his hands, arms, back, buttocks and thighs. No positive identification was made of the shark. All that was known was that it was between ten and twelve feet long.

The next day, when the story broke in the newspapers and wire services across the country, it immediately stirred up controversy over the old question of whether a shark would deliberately attack a human being. In northwest Florida the question was: Had this shark intentionally attacked, or was it a case of mistaken identity?

The Dolphin Skindiving Club members felt that it had been a case of mistaken identity. They said that Grover, attired in his black rubber diving suit, would have been extremely difficult to identify in the dark water; that the circumstances of the bloody and dark waters, the proximity of the shark, Grover's unloaded gun and the cobia breaking loose from the spear were highly coincidental. The odds were against such an accident being repeated.

When details of the attack were examined by authorities, their findings indicated just how coincidental it had been.

Was it a coincidence that the shark was in the area when the scent of blood and the wounded fish drove him to attack? Or had he been lurking in the background all the time?

Very little is known about cobia, which the divers were hunting, but one fact was clear: "The migratory species commonly travels in the company of large sharks," said Dr. C. Richard Robins of the Institute of Marine Science at the University of Miami. "This is not an invariable association, but it certainly comes as no surprise that a shark would be in the vicinity of the cobias. If there is any real relationship between these two animals, and there seems to be, it is the cobia that travels with the shark and not the reverse." This could explain the shark's presence moments after Grover shot his second cobia.

Did the shark know it was attacking a human being?

Ichthyologist Luis R. Rivas of the Department of Zoology at the University of Miami thought it unlikely. "I believe it was a case of mistaken identity brought about by the bleeding cobia," he said. The attack took place under unfavorable conditions: the sky was cloudy; the water unclear. A diver wearing a black rubber suit and doubling up on the surface could have been mistaken for a floundering and wounded fish.

Neither authority thought it possible for the victim to pry open the jaws of a determined shark the size of the one described. "The release must have been voluntary on the part of the shark, perhaps in response to the boy's efforts," said Dr. Robins. The fact that the shark did not follow up the attack once the victim was released seemed to substantiate this.

Ernest Grover survived his shark attack, an attack in which he had apparently been the victim of circumstances, an accident which many said would never happen again. But three months later, less than seven miles from where Grover was attacked, it did happen again. And this time the victim was not so fortunate.

On August 15, Bill Redmon, Jr., took a party of skindivers seven to eight miles off the Panama City beaches to a favorite fishing and diving spot called the Warsaw Hole. It was a fine day. The sky was clear and there was just enough wind to ruffle the surface. One of the members of the five-man group was twenty-six-year-old James C. Neal, an Army lieutenant attached to Fort Rucker, Alabama.

When the party reached their destination they anchored their boat and dropped a shot line down through seventy-three feet of clear blue water to the coral rocks below. Donning scuba gear, the five divers armed themselves with spearguns and made their way down the line on a brief exploratory hunt. When they returned to the boat a few minutes later hardly a man failed to come back without a good catch. Lieutenant Neal brought up a fine fish. After a while the divers went down the line again. On the bottom they separated to hunt the reef. Later, when they returned to the boat, Neal was missing.

Gary Seymour, a member of the Dolphin Skindivers, who was diving nearby, remembered that he had seen Neal on the reef and at the time he was swimming toward the shot line twenty-five or thirty feet away where the other divers were grouped.

"I never saw him again," Seymour said. There was no indication that any of the other divers saw the officer again either.

"I went on down the reef," Seymour continued. "killing several snappers and groupers. Then I met Jeff Sherman, who wrote 'SHARK' on the bottom and described it as a ten-footer." A few minutes later Sherman shot a large jewfish, and when the pair of divers surfaced to boat the catch they learned that everyone was present except Neal. Seymour, Sherman and Lee Larson immediately went down to look for him. Minutes later Seymour found himself in trouble.

"I was going along the reef with a string of fish tied to my belt," he said. "A big shark passed by about three feet away, and I made a fuss in the water to scare him away. Then another shark came from behind and missed me by about six inches. I'm sure it was a mako. The other could have been a blue or a gray shark. Both sharks made passes at me, and I backed against the rocks so I had only to watch in front of me." Seymour inched his way along the reef toward the shot line until he met Sherman and Larson, then the trio came up.

Realizing that Neal had now been missing longer than his air supply would have permitted, the divers buoyed the spot and went for help. Two helicopters from Tyndall Field and the U. S. Air Mine Development Unit, as well as a crash boat and two rescue vessels, searched the area for several hours. A dozen skindivers searched the sea but did not stay long in the water because of a report from one of the divers that the area was heavily infested with sharks.

The next day Navy divers from the U. S. Navy Mine Defense Laboratory systematically searched the reef. They found—scattered over a wide area three hundred yards from where he disappeared —Neal's face mask, speargun, canvas gloves, torn rubber swim fins, pieces of the lead-weight belt he had worn about his waist, a knife in scabbard and parts of his shredded swimming trunks and undershirt. The scraps of clothing bore traces of blood and all the equipment was deeply scarred with slash marks unquestionably made by the teeth of large sharks.

No one will ever know with any certainty what happened to Lieutenant James C. Neal as he swam along the reef by himself, but all evidence indicates that he suddenly became the target of a savage shark attack and was consumed by one or more sharks.

For Flordia the tragic events of 1959 finally came to an end on September 25 when Robert Walker, twenty-nine, and James Plouff, forty-five, went fishing in a small boat three miles out in the Atlantic off Port Everglades. At 4 P.M. the boat's outboard motor ran out of gas. As the anglers were refueling it, a large wave overturned their boat. Plouff grabbed a boat cushion as he went into the water but the currents swept him away. Walker hung onto the boat until it sank, then clutched one of the floating life cushions.

These torn and tooth-scarred effects are all that were found of skindiver Lt. James C. Neal who was the victim of a vicious shark attack near Panama City, Florida, in 1959.

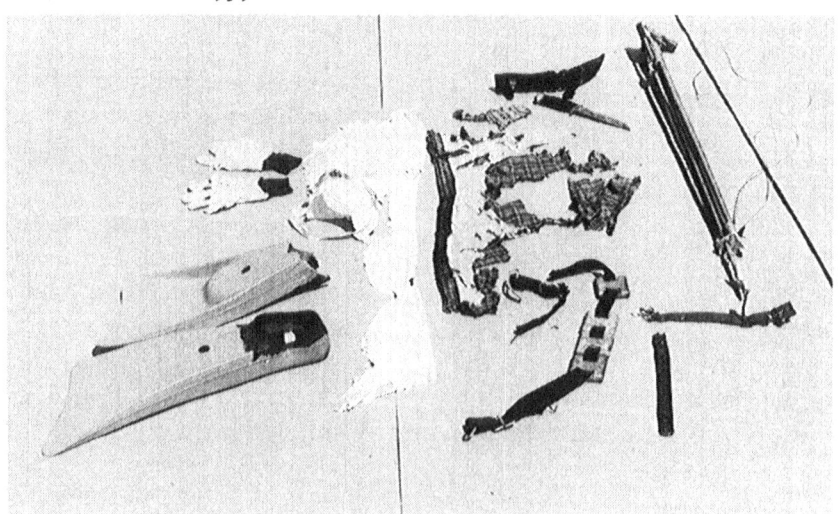

For Plouff, drifting in the cold water, the night was comparatively uneventful except for being the most miserable one he had ever spent in his life. But for Walker, the night was a harrowing nightmare. Not long after darkness fell, he realized to his horror that he was not alone in the water. At first there was only movement around him, then a shark bumped him. With the next surge he felt something tug at his clothes. Finally the shark bit him on both hands, dragging him five feet underwater. After Walker shook his attacker loose it returned twice, the second time accompanied by ten other sharks, which he tried to fend off by kicking at them. First one shark, then another attacked him. This continued throughout the night.

By noon the following day, Plouff, who had been unmolested, was rescued by a charter boat that immediately radioed the news to the Coast Guard. The message was heard by a man named A. V. Francis on another boat a few miles away. Francis scanned the water and caught sight of the second survivor.

As he pulled the bloody, semiconscious man out of the ocean, the sharks were still circling. Walker was suffering from shock and loss of blood, but he was alive. It was doubtful that he could have survived another hour of the ordeal. At the hospital sixty stitches were required to close wounds on his hands and feet. At least one of the sharks involved in the attack was identified as a hammerhead.

Since then there have been worse years for shark attacks, but 1959 marked the first attempt by scientists to compile a comprehensive, documented record of all shark attacks occurring throughout the world. This project was initiated by the American Institute of Biological Sciences Shark Research Panel, which was formed in 1958 by scientists who were concerned over the lack of dependable information on shark behavior and the scarcity of facts about shark attacks. Its members include Dr. Perry W. Gilbert, Professor of Neurobiology and Behavior at Cornell University, who is chairman of the panel and probably the foremost American authority on sharks; Stewart Springer, Biologist, U. S. Bureau of Commercial Fisheries; Dr. John R. Olive, Executive Director of AIBS; Dr. Sidney R. Galler, Assistant Secretary for Science at the Smithsonian Institution; Dr. Albert L. Tester, Senior Professor of Zoology, University of Hawaii; Deane Holt, Biologist, Office of Naval Research; and Dr. Leonard P. Schultz, Curator of Fishes for the Smithsonian Institution.

For the last eleven years this panel has been engaged in documenting facts concerning all known shark attacks, and has carried on shark research programs designed to find out why sharks behave as they do. Here are some of the facts revealed by the Shark Attack File for 1959:

A. Of the world's thirty-six unprovoked and three provoked attacks on man, one third of these were fatal.

B. Only two unprovoked attacks occurred in water colder than 70° F, which tends to support the theory that shark activity is greatly reduced, if not almost nonexistent, below this temperature range; however, so is the public's normal bathing and skindiving activities.

C. Twice as many people were attacked by sharks after 1:00 P.M. as opposed to the morning or night hours. Again this is a reflection of the increased number of swimmers during this time.

D. Five out of twelve bathers attacked in 1959 were swimming alone or at a distance from their companions. This emphasizes the long recommended safety rule: "Never swim or dive alone."

E. Three of the nine divers attacked while spearfishing or diving for shellfish were attacked on the surface—the area generally agreed as the danger zone for a diver because there his movements are less likely to be rhythmic and coordinated. Two were towing wounded fish, which is considered an added inducement to attack.

F. Male victims outnumbered female victims twelve to one. This does not mean that sharks exhibited any preference, only that men entered the domain of sharks more frequently than women.

G. All but six attacks took place between 35° N latitude and 35° S latitude, well within the world's shark attack belt. January was the worst month for attacks south of the equator, and August was the worst month in northern latitudes.

H. A total of thirteen unprovoked attacks, five fatal, occurred in Australian waters. Twelve unprovoked attacks, five fatal, took place in United States and Mexican waters. South America ranked third in 1959 with four attacks, one of which was fatal.

3

Sharks Out of the Past

The shark—primitive, deadly, mysterious monarch of the sea—where did it come from? What manner of prehistoric creature from the forgotten past spawned it? How did it weather eons of environmental change and still survive?

To answer these questions we would have to look down the long corridor of time into the abysmal past. We would have to see things on earth as they were long before the origin of man, who, as *Homo sapiens*, is believed to have appeared on earth barely a million years ago. We would have to look beyond the birth of our mightiest mountain ranges—the Andes, the Alps, the Himalayas, the Rockies —which were thrust into existence some seventy million years ago. We would have to look far beyond all these things to a point in geological time called the Devonian Period, which began about 405 million years ago and ended about 345 million years ago. And there, in shallow Devonian seas, we would find the ancient ancestors of our present-day shark.

The Age of Fishes had already arrived some twenty million years earlier during the Silurian Period, but by Devonian time the first shark-like creatures were already well developed. This early form was called *Cladoselache*. It looked much like our sharks of today, with broad, well-developed paired fins, sharp dagger-like teeth, a streamlined body, a skeleton of cartilage and open gill slits. Its maximum length was about four feet. All sharks—both past and present —have lacked bony skeletons. Since cartilage is a flexible, gristle-like substance, it was easily destroyed by the ravages of times. For that reason paleontologists have found only the scantest fossil evidence of early sharks, and this often consists only of a few teeth and an occasional dorsal spine. However, one of the most valuable records of a prehistoric shark was found in Ohio at a geological site called the Cleveland Shales. There, amongst late Devonian fossils, paleontologists uncovered the delicate impressions and body outline of *Cladoselache*, complete in such detail as to show imprints of its muscles and kidneys.

The *Cladoselache* became extinct sometime during the Parmian Period (280 to 230 million years ago). It was replaced by an evolutionary form called the Hybodont, which had two kinds of specialized teeth and more refined fins that were narrow-based and flexible, as are those of today's sharks. The Hybodonts eventually gave way to more improved shark forms, but at least two of their direct descendants are alive today—the Port Jackson and the frilled sharks.

Modern sharks began their development in the late Jurassic period, about 150 million years ago. This was the time when *Brontosaurus*, the sixty-seven-foot-long herbivorous dinosaur, roamed Jurassic swamps along with such creatures as the twenty-foot-long armored *Stegosaurus*. During this period sharks were a modified version of the earlier Hybodonts. The chief difference was a jaw structure in which the upper portion was supported by a modified gill arch and not hinged directly to the skull—an arrangement that permitted it to move forward while feeding. These sharks formed many families, and by the close of the Miocene Period, twenty-six to twelve million years ago, ancestors of every family of shark we know today, from the dogfish to the whale shark, flourished in Miocene seas. Relics of these early sharks are numerous and wide-spread across the country.

In 1853 a geologist for the Pacific Railway Survey found several shark teeth in a parched California hill more than a hundred miles from the sea. . . . In the soil of a Parke County Indiana farm fossil hunters found the teeth of large sharks that had been trapped in a shallow saline basin. . . . In the small town of Mulberry in south central Florida a pebble phosphate miner collected a shoebox full of fossil shark teeth the size of his hand. . . . And in northwest Florida's Chipola River skindivers find hundreds of fossil shark teeth a day.

These teeth are all that remain of our more recent shark ancestors—those that lived about twenty million years ago. The 1853 California find unveiled what is now known as Sharktooth Hill, an area about seven miles northeast of Bakersfield, California, that has long been a fertile hunting ground for avid shark-tooth collectors. According to paleontologists, a prehistoric sea called the Temblor once covered this area to a depth of two hundred feet. As it receded, some twenty million years ago, it left the primeval ooze rich with the remains of whales, porpoises, dolphins, sea cows, seals, sea lions and at least twenty-five species of sharks—including one monstrous member 120 feet long. The length of this shark was determined by its enormous teeth, which measured nearly six inches long and weighed twelve ounces apiece. Our largest sharks today have teeth no longer than two inches. The giant teeth belonged to *Carcharodon*, an ancestor of our present-day great white, or man-eater, shark. When the American Museum of Natural History reconstructed the gigantic jaws of this prehistoric shark, they were large enough to easily accommodate six standing men. Similar huge teeth of *Carcharodon* have turned up in geological sites at Staten Island, New York, the Calvert Cliffs on the western shore of Chesapeake Bay and in three Florida locations: the Chipola River near Marianna, sixty miles west of Tallahassee; on the beach at Venice, fifteen miles south of Sarasota; and in the pebble phosphate mines at Bartow, thirty-nine miles east of Tampa.

Fossil teeth of less prodigious size are common. In size and shape they resemble arrowheads, but in the geological sites where they are found, they are decidedly more numerous. This fact has attracted many amateur fossil hunters who spend weekends and vacations shark-tooth sleuthing in such varied places as the plains of central Kansas, in Wyoming, Idaho, New Mexico, New Jersey, South Carolina, New York and Maryland. In Alabama cotton fields shark teeth had been unearthed among the fossilized bones of *Zeuglodon*, a prehistoric whale that grew to seventy feet and may have been a prey for sharks. In Florida's Apalachicola River headwaters, 105 miles from the Gulf of Mexico, fossil shark teeth have been found with holes drilled in them by Indians who apparently wore them as pendants. At Venice, Florida, the teeth appear as small, ebony-black triangles in the sand. Whole specimens are not easily found in that area, since it has long been picked over by legions of tooth-hunting tourists. At Bartow, however, large tracts of ground have been broken in this pebble phosphate mining area and wherever this occurs motorists find shark teeth and other fossil fragments exposed almost at roadside.

(37)

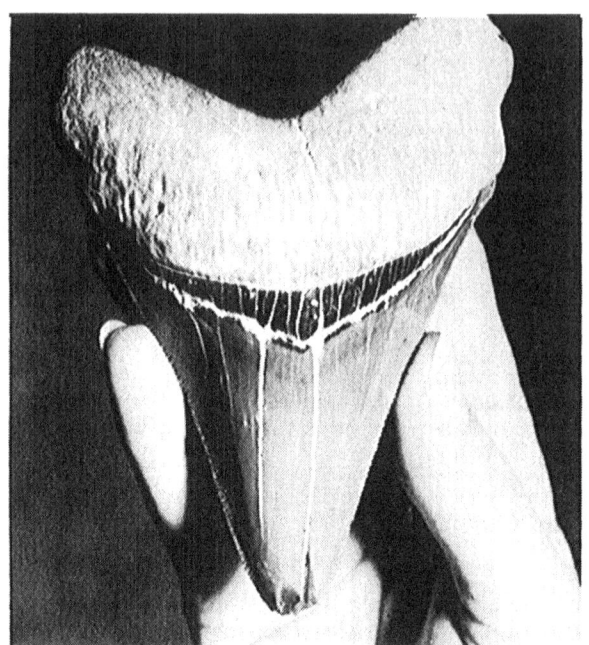

This giant shark tooth came from Carcharodon, *a 90-foot prehistoric ancestor of the Great White shark. The fossil tooth is from 12 to 26 million years old. Many are found throughout the United States. This one came from the Pebble Phosphate pits near Bartow, Florida.*

The different shapes, sizes and colors make fossil shark teeth unusual collector's items. Many are sold and traded by fossil hunters, while others are made into unique jewelry. After all, how many people can say that they own pins, earrings, tie tacs or cuff links made from the teeth of a twenty-million-year-old sea monster?

Although fossil teeth are virtually all that remain of the forebearers of our present shark population, today's sharks are frequently called "living fossils" because that is exactly what they are—living relics from the past. In the beginning, while the seas and continents of our world were changing, the sharks were there. While countless forms of life came into existence, lived out their specialized lives through millions of years, then passed into extinction, the sharks remained. While continents rose and fell, while much of the world's climate changed from tropical to arctic with the coming of Ice Age glaciers that lasted thousands of years, the sharks still remained. And when this environment finally changed back to the conditions we know today, the sharks continue to remain. The question is: How did they survive when so many other seemingly more capable forms of life perished?

The answer to this question has been pieced together by scientists who have been able to study the environmental changes of the past and how they affected the animals that existed through these periods. At one time the skies were dominated by *Pteranodons*, a toothless, long-beaked, hammer-headed flying reptile with a twenty-five-foot wingspan, the largest animal ever to fly. Yet, it became extinct. So did such big-boned giants as *Tyrannosaurus rex*, the largest carnivorous dinosaur; the woolly mammoth; the saber-toothed cat and thousands of other animals including what was probably the scourge of Devonian seas—*Dinichthys*, a giant, thirty-foot armor-plated predator fish that swam in the same waters as the first small primitive sharks. All of these creatures were highly developed and specialized. They had adapted to their environment.

But when new mountain ranges rose and altered the climate, the environment changed. Landlocked bodies of water gradually dried up. Aquatic species that could not develop into amphibians soon perished. Survival in the overpopulated seas became limited to the fiercest fish, the swiftest swimmers. The heavily bone-plated denizens soon fell victims of lighter, more mobile predators. These in turn fed upon each other until only the strongest survived. On land, similar changes took place. Food became scarce. Animals that required specialized diets probably expired first. Others could have left the country for greener pastures elsewhere, but they proved too big to travel. Since they could neither change their environment nor adapt to it, they died. They were what scientists call too highly specialized —too completely adapted for a special kind of life.

The animals that survived—and there were many, both on land and sea—did so because they were able to adjust to new environments. This is why the shark survived. Even today its remarkable ability to fit itself completely into abnormal surroundings is exemplified by at least one species—the Lake Nicaragua shark that has adapted itself to life in fresh water.

No one knows for sure how this phenomenon began, but many scientists think that it may have happened this way: from two thousand to five thousand years ago, the area now known as Lake Nicaragua in Central America is believed to have been a salt-water bay that fronted on the Pacific Ocean. Sharks entered and left the bay freely. But sometime during this period violent volcanic eruptions suddenly sealed off the bay from the ocean, trapping a number of sharks and several other salt-water species there. As rivers flowed into the lake it gradually became fresh water. The marine fish adapted themselves to this new environment and survived.

What lends substance to this theory is a string of twenty-three volcanoes, many of them active, that run down the western side of Nicaragua. Geological evidence indicates that there was considerable earth-altering volcanic activity during the time the lake was supposedly formed. And local inhabitants readily vouch for the fact that the sharks are there, along with the sawfish, tarpon and remoras, which have all adapted. The Lake Nicaragua shark, once designated as a separate species, is now believed to be identical to the cub or bull shark (*Carcharhinus leucas*) commonly found in our coastal waters. Yet the fresh-water variety has earned the reputation of being uncommonly voracious. Natives claim that at least one person a year loses his life to this man-eater. But, oddly enough, the salt-water version of this shark is believed to be less inclined to attacks upon humans, despite its probably greater opportunities. Bull sharks, however, are still regarded as one of our more dangerous species.

Lake Nicaragua's only connection to salt water is the twisting, rapids-filled, 130-mile long San Juan River, which flows into the Caribbean. Until recently most scientists have discounted this treacherous waterway as a route for sharks to enter the lake from the sea. But now some are not so certain, and at least one scientist is presently conducting research at Lake Nicaragua that may solve the riddle.

Several species of sharks are known to be able to travel in and out of fresh-water tributaries with no apparent ill effect. Although bull sharks are particularly adroit at this, sharp-nose sharks have been identified a few miles up the Mississippi River; a species called the river shark commonly enters the waterways of South Africa and has been caught 120 miles up the Zambezi River; and perhaps the most ferocious river-runner of all, the Ganges River shark, has caused many deaths in the coastal-linked rivers of India. Reports throughout the world indicate that many sharks have been sighted in many rivers but, as so often is true, few of these species are accurately identified. All of which points out that the shark's easy adaptability is but another intriguing facet of this particularly fascinating animal from out of the past.

4

Anatomy of a Shark

What are the odds for or against one of us becoming a victim of this creature's savage attack the next time we go to the beach? Unfortunately, the shark experts cannot give us a perfectly satisfactory answer to this question yet. But they do assure us that the odds *against* our being attacked are extremely long. Perhaps millions to one. In 1959, which was the first year records were kept on shark attacks, there were thirty-nine attacks in the entire world. In an extremely bad shark year there are not more than one hundred attacks on man throughout the world and approximately half of these are fatal. By comparison, more than three times as many people in the United States alone will die from bee stings or lightning.

In other words, you could swim in any sea, any ocean or any body of water in the world where sharks live and do so with far less risk than you run every time you take a trip in an automobile. Despite this fact, we attach a sinister, overpowering fear to the thought that in the very water where we swim there also lurks an animal fully capable of eating us alive. As with all frightening things we fear most what we understand the least. And since sharks are not only fearsome beasts but also some of the least understood of all creatures, then our fear of them is often equally distorted far out of proportion. The sight of any large shadowy fish cruising along a beach can strike immediate awe and doubt in the viewer's mind. The sight of any curved dark fin slicing the water's surface can strike instant terror and fear in the bravest of men, whether that fin belongs, in fact, to nothing more dangerous than a playful porpoise or is indeed the dorsal fin of a passing shark. The outcry "Shark!" can stampede a beach full of bathers, while the mere rumor that one has been sighted is sufficient to create unfounded apprehension in all who hear it.

If modern man were not becoming more involved with the sea perhaps the shark would remain the sinister, unknown and feared creature it has always been. But man *is* concerning himself more and more with the sea. He is doing it from necessity. For we realize now that there will come a day when the earth's soil will no longer support all of us. Our last great untapped resource on earth is the ocean bottom and the sea, which comprises 71 percent of the world's surface. Unless man can learn to exploit this vast watery region, he may perish.

For years now divers in growing numbers have begun searching the ocean's depths for oil, metals and other hidden resources. Dedicated men such as Edwin A. Link and Jacques-Yves Cousteau, the father of modern-day diving, are pioneering new ways to farm the ocean floor, planning and designing sea-bottom communities that will someday enable man to live and work in self-contained cities beneath the sea. Exploration of our world's watery "inner space" is progressing with the same determined desire for knowledge that exists in our quest to explore outer space. But as man advances into the sea he is being confronted by his age-old enemy, the shark. In order to cope with this enemy we must know more about him. Scientists are far from knowing all there is to know about sharks. But what they already know and what they are rapidly learning is shedding new light on a creature that has been shrouded in mystery for centuries.

Sharks and rays belong to the group of vertebrates called the *Elasmobranchii*, which means they possess skeletons of cartilage (gristle) and five to seven pairs of gill openings. The entire family, which not only includes sharks and rays but also several species such as sawfish and guitarfish that appear to be links between the two, are called Selachians. They range in size from a few inches long at maturity to some sixty feet long. There are about 250 species of sharks inhabiting the waters of the world and about thirty-five of these are potentially dangerous to man. Unlike other fish, the shark does not have a bone in its body. Its skeleton is composed entirely of the flexible, gristle-like substance called cartilage. Although sharks resemble bony fish in some ways, their method of reproduction is more like that of the higher mammals—at least in the primary stages. The male shark is equipped with a pair of reproductive organs called claspers. These appendages are located on the inner edges of the pelvic fins. At mating time the male and female meet and the male inserts the claspers into the female organ called the cloaca. In less than a half hour the breeding is completed and the sharks swim their separate ways.

All Selachians produce their young in the manner common to their species. Some sharks are viviparous, nurturing the young in their wombs and giving birth to live offspring as do dogs, cats, cattle or man. Others are ovoviviparous, forming eggs that are hatched *within* the mother, who then gives birth to live young. Still others are oviparous in that they lay eggs from which the young are hatched.

Most sharks fall into the first two categories and give birth to live young, which are commonly called pups. The offspring vary in size from two to three inches for the chain dogfish to five to six feet in length for the basking shark. But most average from twelve to twenty-four inches long for the common species. Sharks give birth to their offspring in litters of up to twenty and sometimes more. Each newborn pup is a perfect miniature of the adult. And it arrives in the world with all the shark-like instincts of its parents. In fact it was recently discovered that some sharks are fully capable of exercising these instincts before they even arrive in the world. The sand tiger shark, for example, is a cannibal before it is born. In this species of ovoviviparous shark the eggs are hatched in the mother's uterus, where the young remain until sufficiently developed to enter the ocean. The first baby hatched feeds on its weaker brothers and sisters as they emerge from their eggs. Since there are two separate uteruses, two young sand tigers survive to be born.

This is the only known case of intra-uterine cannibalism in the animal world. Biologist Stewart Springer discovered the remarkable process the hard way. As he was examining a pregnant shark an unborn baby bit his hand!

Sharks share no love or affection for their offspring, and if given the opportunity they will quickly make a meal of them. The young pups are on their own from the very beginning, fighting and fending for themselves. In all respects they are one of the most unique creatures the world has ever known.

From the day they are born until the day they die most sharks

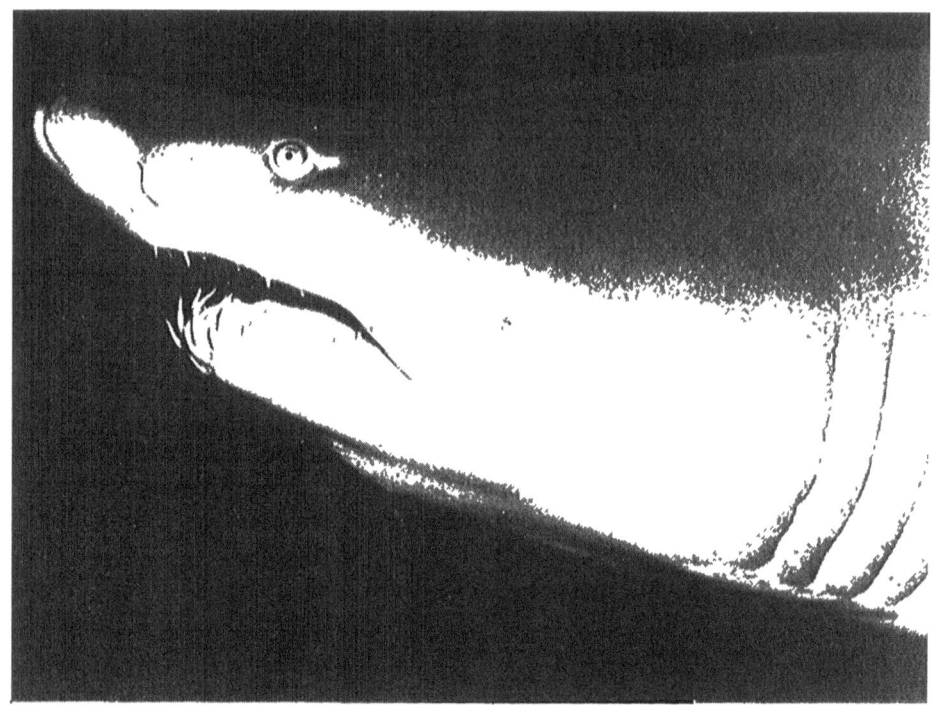

The sand tiger shark is as dangerous as it is ugly.

must swim constantly to stay alive. There are two reasons for this. One is that, lacking an air bladder, they must swim or they will sink. But this is not the primary reason they must keep moving. In all but the most sluggish species, such as nurse sharks (*Ginglymostoma cirratum*), this movement, or some other means, is required to force water into their mouths and through their gill clefts so that they can absorb oxygen to "breathe." Sharks swim by a serpentine undulation of their powerfully muscular bodies. The sweeping movements of their caudal fins or tails provide most of this power. Their forward or pectoral fins are large and fairly rigid, serving as wing-like stabilizers for maneuvering and possibly for some support in the water mass. Sharks are incapable of backing up. So if something should prevent this forward progress they are unable to ventilate their gills and soon die. Shark nets protecting Australian and South African beaches have proved effective because of this principle. When sharks blunder into the nets and become enmeshed they can neither move forward nor back up. They soon "drown" from lack of oxygen.

Our nurse sharks and a few of the other bottom-dwelling species may lie dormant for long periods of time because they can pump water through their respiratory systems by fanning their gill slits. Moving currents probably assist in this function, enabling various species of coastal sharks, including tiger sharks, to rest or at least temporarily cease their activities. But on the whole, sharks never sleep in the way that we know it. The pelagic species—those that spend their entire lives in the open ocean—are deprived of any resting place. To stop swimming would send them plummeting into the abysmal depths. Whatever sharks do that corresponds to this restorative pause that we call sleep must occur while they are swimming.

Despite a shark's weight—and some weigh in excess of several thousand pounds—they seem to require little movement to keep themselves buoyant. The secret lies in the size and contents of a shark's liver. This huge organ makes up as much as a quarter of the owner's weight, and is rich in oil. Since oil is lighter than water, the shark's liver plays a role similar to the air bladders of other fish in helping to maintain buoyancy. Recent investigations by Dr. C. Scott Johnson at the Mote Marine Laboratory in Sarasota, Florida, revealed these surprising facts: sharks have a different sort of weight problem than animals that live on land; the more a shark eats, the lighter it becomes in water; the longer it goes without eating, the heavier it becomes in water.

Think about that for a while and consider how many people would like the shark's problem: eat less to gain weight; eat more to lose weight. Unfortunately, however, sharks are the only creatures able to perform this feat—and it must be done in water. The more food a shark eats, the more oil is produced in its liver, and the lighter the shark becomes in water. In research programs presently in progress investigators are adding lead weights to a shark in captivity. This artificially creates the same effect of a shark in a starved condition. By doing this and observing the shark's swimming performance, researchers can learn how greatly the shark's weight in water can be allowed to increase and still allow him to swim efficiently. If the scientists then measure the rate at which the shark uses the oil stored in its liver as nourishment, they can estimate how long a shark can go without eating. And this in turn may be of important significance in understanding more about sharks and why they attack.

Nature has perfectly designed sharks for the element in which they live. From the tip of their wedge-shaped snouts down their taper-

The business end of a Great White or Man-eater shark.

ing bodies to the tip of their tails, they are the ultimate in stream-lining. And they are armed literally from head to tail with teeth. The shark's cartilaginous jaws are lined with hundreds of triangular or spike-shaped, razor-sharp teeth. As many as five rows lie back flat inside the jaws beneath folds of the gum. They are reserves for the outer one or two rows that stand upright around the rim of the jaws ready for use. When one of these teeth is lost or damaged, a reserve tooth moves up to replace it. These teeth are formidable weapons, capable of removing ten pounds of flesh from a victim in a single bite. And the power behind that bite is awesome. Contrary to popular belief, sharks need not roll on their sides to feed. Although their mouths are located several inches back from the underside of their snouts, they can attack head-on. This is because their upper jaws are not fused to their brain cases but can be raised and protruded for biting. At the Lerner Marine Laboratory on Bimini in the Bahama Islands, scientists have made underwater films of sharks feeding on a dead marlin to understand more about how they bite. The shark propels itself straight into its target, mouth agap. The lower jaw sinks its teeth first, the protruded upper jaw follows. The shark violently shakes its entire body and tears out a mouthful of meat, leaving a ragged, crescent-shaped hole the size of a watermelon.

In Australia, where shark attacks occur with tragic frequency, doctors noted that the victims often suffered abrasions that were not caused by the shark's bite. These wounds were made by contacts with the shark's body, which is covered with "skin teeth." These are tiny, spiky protuberances called placoid scales or dermal denticles. They have all the attributes of teeth. Each spike is covered with dentine and has a central pulp canal containing a nerve and blood vessels. These skin teeth are set at an angle in a shark's hide, so that you could rub your hand along a shark's flank from head to tail and feel little resistance. But try rubbing your hand in the opposite direction and it will not move. The dermal denticles hold it as tightly as the teeth of a rasp. Sharks often bump a victim before attacking. They may do this out of curiosity or caution. But against bare skin this sideswipe can be severe enough to draw blood and trigger a more direct assault.

The shark has aptly been nicknamed a "swimming nose." The scent of fish oil or blood in the water has the same effect upon it as a red cape waved in front of a fighting bull. When sharks smell these odors in the water they are triggered into abrupt, unrestrained fits of excitement, during which they may swim about rapidly and erratically, snapping and biting at anything within reach, including other sharks. This behavior is called a feeding frenzy. It is at its worst when a pack of sharks is involved. And it is this kind of uncontrolled activity that is most dreaded by survivors of sea disasters.

The shark's sense of smell is so acute that it can detect these odors in water as much as a quarter of a mile away. Despite the fact that a shark's brain is relatively small, seldom larger than three inches for even the largest species, it was obviously designed more for smell-

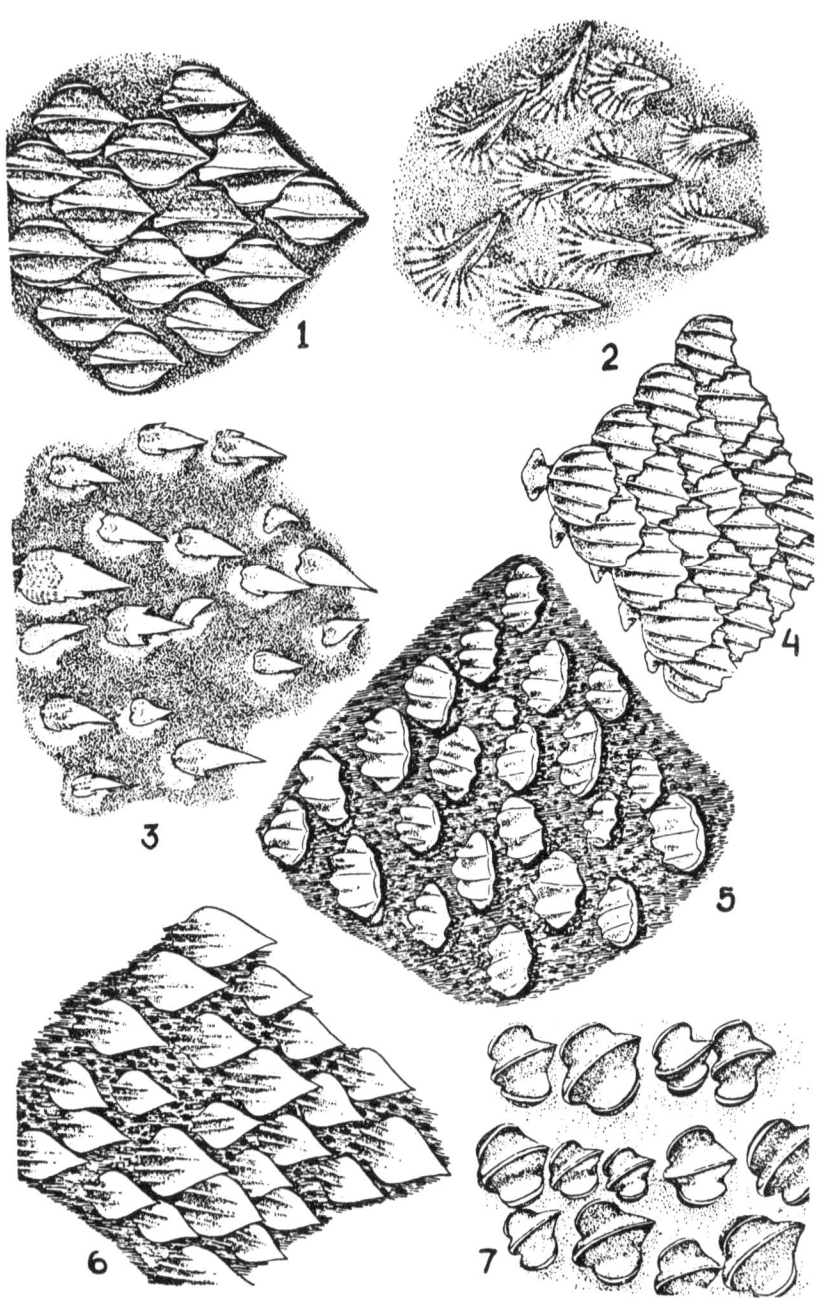

The denticles or "skin teeth" of sharks vary with different species. Under a microscope they appear as above: (1) Tiger shark; (2) Basking shark; (3) Cat shark; (4) Thresher shark; (5) Brown shark; (6) Smooth dogfish; (7) Sand, or Sand Tiger shark. These sharp placoid scales are what cause abrasion wounds on victims of a shark attack.

ing than for reasoning. It has the shape of a wishbone. What would correspond to the right and left forks of the wishbone are the shark's well-developed olfactory lobes, which interpret what it smells. These are linked directly to its nostrils on either side of its broad head. If a shark picks up a scent in one nostril it turns in that direction until it detects it in the other, then it turns back again. In this manner a shark swims a serpentine course back along the trail of scent until it finds the source. Sport fishermen capitalize on the shark's ability to follow the faintest scent for great distances by throwing handfuls of oily ground fish into the water to entice sharks to their hooks. The scent of this chum line will travel for miles on a strong current, and the sharks find it hard to resist.

Almost as acute is the shark's sense of hearing. Sounds are transmitted to them as low frequency vibrations, which travel extremely well in water. These vibrations can be made by the flurries of a school of fish, the flutterings of a wounded fish, the splashing of a sea mammal or human. Frequently they are the sounds of an animal in distress. The shark picks up these signals by its remarkable lateralis system. This is a network of fluid-filled pores supplied with nerves that lie along both sides of its body and are connected to a special center in the shark's brain. Exactly how far the shark can hear with this system is still a matter of conjecture, but underwater explosions or the sound of any ship or plane disaster at sea apparently can attract sharks from considerable distances. The snout and entire body of a shark contain a variety of sensing pores, but scientists do not yet know why or how a shark uses them. Some may be capable of interpreting physical characteristics of the water such as greater or less salt content, which might affect the shark's internal system or its buoyancy. Other pores may be electrical receptors capable of detecting kinetic electrical emissions given off by moving prey, thus helping the shark to home in on victims that it cannot see. Although this is pure speculation and scientists can as yet only theorize on the possibilities, they do know that these sensor pores that cover a shark's body are there for some very definite purpose.

It has long been believed that sharks have poor eyesight. Experiments with them over the last few years have proved this incorrect. Visual acuity may be the least developed of their senses, but their eyesight is sharp enough to allow them to rely upon it within one hundred feet of their prey. This distance varies according to water

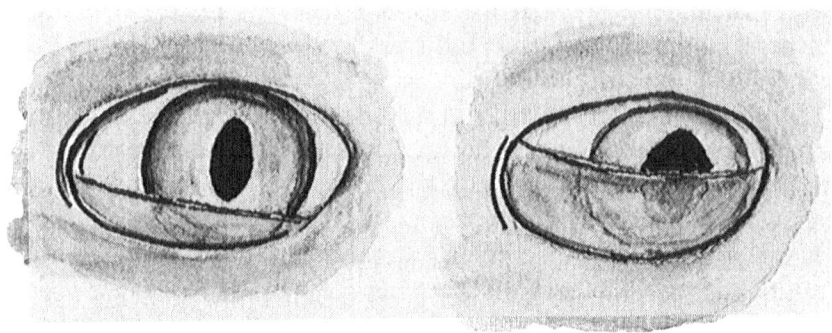

The nictitating membrane on some shark's eyes acts as a translucent eyelid that moves upward from the bottom, shielding and protecting the eyes. The illustration shows the reaction of a Lemon shark's blink to a beam of light. As the membrane closes, the pupil responds to the darkness by expanding (right). Birds and reptiles also possess these membranes.

clarity and the species of shark involved. Some sharks have extremely small eyes for the size of their bodies, while others, living at greater depths where light is poor, may have unusually large eyes. Species that specialize in feeding at night have light-reflecting tissues behind their retinas similar to those that make cats' eyes glow ghost-like in the beam of a headlight. These reflective surfaces help animals see in the dark by gathering and intensifying what little light exists. In the same way, these reflective surfaces give sharks night vision in murky or dark waters. This is one reason why swimming at night in the ocean can be extremely dangerous.

The eyes of certain sharks contain nictitating membranes, which form a kind of translucent eyelid that moves upward from the bottom of the eye. The purpose of the membrane is to protect and clean the eye. It also serves to cut down glare and allow the shark to see better when it is near the surface. This novel eyelid—found also in birds and reptiles—acts both as a built-in windshield wiper and sunglasses for the animal possessing it.

Can sharks detect colors? This question has long puzzled scientists. At one time it was thought that sharks were color blind, a belief based on the apparent lack of color-perceiving cones in sharks' eyes. But recently these cones have been discovered in some sharks' eyes. Whether or not they see colors as humans do is still open for debate. Scientists know that sharks can differentiate between colors, but they believe that this is a response to reflectivity, or brightness, rather than to color itself.

Do sharks feel pain as warm-blooded animals do? Most authorities are doubtful that any cold-blooded animal, which includes all fish, have any sense of pain. There are numerous cases on record of sharks being shot, hauled aboard a fishing vessel, split open and the carcass tossed overboard, only to have the shark swim off and continue feeding again. One angler caught a shark, "killed" it with a bullet through the head from a .30–.30 rifle and fifteen minutes later caught the same shark again on another bait. The bullet had apparently only stunned it.

Sharks die slowly. In the meantime they seem capable of withstanding a considerable amount of physical damage. Medical doctors are interested in knowing how they accomplish this.

It has long been believed that sharks not only eat just about anything but that their appetites seem to have no limits. Yet sharks in captivity have gone on hunger strikes for days, weeks and months without any apparent ill effects. What was not known until recently is that some sharks can exist without eating for as long as a year! They do this by living off the stored oil in their livers much in the same way hibernating bears live through the winters by metabolizing the fat of their bodies. But why sharks in their natural environment may cease feeding for long periods of time to utilize this oil is presently being studied in research programs at the Mote Marine Laboratory in Florida.

The digestive system of a shark is in itself unique. It has the capacity to store items for days or weeks without digesting them, while simultaneously digesting other items. A shark can regurgitate at will whatever displeases it. For that matter it can even voluntarily turn its stomach inside out and evert it, spit it out so that it extends beyond the shark's jaw, then gulp it down again. Shark fishermen have seen them resort to this tactic in an effort to free themselves from an offending hook in their stomachs. Yet, as amazing as these antics seem, the shark's digestive tract is an exceedingly primitive one that apparently ceased evolving at an early stage of development. The stomach is little more than a holding pouch where some, but not a great deal, of the digestion begins. It is in a cigar-shaped appendage just below the stomach where the real digestion occurs, and this organ, called the spiral-valve intestine, may hold the secret of how

A sight guaranteed to quicken a swimmer's heartbeat—a cruising 12-foot 1,015-pound Tiger shark. This is an uncharacteristic attitude for despite fiction and myth, sharks seldon swim with their dorsal fins out of water.

sharks maintain a "selective" stomach. The cigar-shaped intestine is comparatively short, about twelve inches long in some sharks, but it contains an inner structure resembling a spiral staircase. Without this, food would pass rapidly through the organ without being wholly absorbed. But because of the spiral structure, food is slowly spiraled around the valve while strong gastric juices liberally lashed with hydrochloric acid break it down. During this process the intestinal walls absorb everything of value and wastes are ejected at the end of the spiral.

In *Shadows in the Sea*, McCormick, Allen and Young site interesting examples of how sharks can store food for long periods of time. A fourteen-foot tiger shark was caught in Australia and kept in captivity. It lived a month, during which it was fed only horsemeat. In its stomach when it died were found two four-foot dolphin fish that it had stored undigested throughout its captivity. In another instance a tiger shark's stomach contained thirty-two fish fifteen inches long, neatly packed and undigested. Yet a shark's digestive juices are strong enough to eat the varnish off a boat deck.

The amount and variety of absolutely indigestible items often found in a shark's stomach is legend. Tiger sharks are especially noted for being the "junk collectors" of the clan. The odd assortment of items found in one tiger's stomach included, among other things: three overcoats, a raincoat and a driver's license, plus a pair of old pants, a pair of shoes, a cow's hoof, the horns of a deer, twelve undigested lobsters and a chicken coop with a few feathers and bones left inside! Another was found to have consumed a keg of nails, a roll of tar paper and a carpenter's square. Everything except the carpenter.

Why sharks gulp down such indigestible things is something we can only wonder about, for no one has ever found a reason. Some believe that sharks that follow ships swallow anything that is dropped or thrown overboard, believing it to be edible. However, at least one scientist has another theory that may prove to be closer to the real reason. At the Mote Marine Laboratory, Captain H. David Baldridge, a Naval biochemist, devised a simple but effective method for weighing sharks under water. In the course of this research he found that a 1,015-pound tiger shark weighed no more than *seven pounds* under water. This remarkable buoyancy was due to the tiger's enormous oil rich liver. Baldridge's studies indicate that it might be possible that a shark could become so buoyant from an excess of liver oil that it would have to expend considerably more effort to dive or maneuver. If this were the case, asks Baldridge, why then would it not be feasible for the shark to cope with the situation as would any good sailor and take on ballast? The added weight of the indigestible junk in a shark's stomach would immediately decrease its buoyancy and give it more maneuverability in the same way that submarines and blimps require slightly negative buoyancy for better control.

On numerous occasions gruesome things have turned up in the stomachs of sharks. Captain William E. Young reported finding the right arm of a man in the stomach of a twelve-foot brown shark that he was skinning. The arm was in a good state of preservation. There were also six fragments of flesh and a twelve by eighteen-inch piece of blue serge cloth in the stomach. Young reported his discovery to a coroner in Key West. Later he learned that a plane had crashed at sea twenty miles from there the day before. A man named Atkins was reported missing. When last seen he had been wearing a blue serge suit.

Years ago, at Pensacola, Florida, a commercial fisherman bought himself a pair of new shoes and went to sea. He never returned. A few days after his disappearance a shark was caught. In its stomach was found a man's leg, the foot of which still wore a new shoe. Both the shoe and the leg were buried as the only remains of the unfortunate fisherman.

In all the annals of crime few murder mysteries have had stranger beginnings or have been solved by more bizarre clues than the one that began on April 17, 1935, in Sydney, Australia. A man named Albert Hobson put out a baited fish line a mile offshore from a popular swimming area called Coogee Beach. Sometime during the night a small shark swallowed the bait and hooked itself. But by morning, when Hobson checked his line, he found a thrashing fourteen-foot tiger shark, which had swallowed the smaller shark and entangled itself in the line.

Hobson dragged the monster ashore and gave it to the nearby Coogee Aquarium. For two days the shark languished near death, but it finally rallied and began eating all the fish thrown to it. Crowds of spectators visited the aquarium daily to see the large shark. Then, a week after its capture, the tiger stopped eating, hardly moved and seemed sick. The next day, while fourteen persons stood at the pool watching, the shark suddenly came to life and went berserk. It raced from one end of the pool to the other, lashing the surface with its tail. Finally it swam in rapid circles, then a brown scum enveloped it. Witnesses were shocked to see emerging out of the cloud and floating eerily to the surface the remains of a rat . . . the body of a sea bird and . . . a human arm with a long rope tied around its wrist.

The gruesome find was taken to the city morgue, where a medical officer examined it. It was the left arm of a muscular man, severed neatly at the shoulder and remarkably well preserved. On the forearm was a tattoo of two boxers confronting each other. The four-foot six-inch rope around its wrist had been tied with a seaman's knot—a clove hitch. A Sydney surgeon and other experts were called in for consultation. Their opinion was that the arm had not been ripped from its owner by a shark, but had been cut away cleanly with a sharp instrument.

The tiger shark was killed, but all its stomach revealed were a few fish bones and the remnants of the small shark it had swallowed on Hobson's line. Sydney police obtained fingerprints from the hand

and traced them to James Smith, a former amateur boxer who was known to have had dealings with the underworld. Further investigation revealed that Smith had been involved in some kind of illegal enterprise with one Reginald William Holmes, a wealthy Sydney boat-builder. He was last seen with a man named Patrick Brady under suspicious enough circumstances to make the police believe that Brady and Holmes had murdered Smith. Brady was picked up for questioning. Four days later Holmes tried to commit suicide but failed. The same day he was released from the hospital he was murdered.

Police pieced together the evidence and came to this conclusion: Smith the boxer had been murdered. In getting rid of the body, the killers for some reason failed to destroy his arm in the same manner. Instead, it was severed from the body. One end of a rope was knotted about its wrist, the other end tied to a weight and it was hurled overboard from a boat. It remained on the bottom of the sea until a small shark gulped it down and later hooked itself on Hobson's line. The big tiger, sensing an easy meal, swallowed the small shark and was in turn caught by Hobson.

The rest of Smith's body was never found. No one was ever convicted of either murder. But it is almost certain that Smith's "avenging arm" returned to point an accusing finger at the guilty. No matter who killed Holmes, Smith's arm brought about his death just as surely as if his finger had pulled the trigger.

5

The Man-eaters

The 250 or more known species of sharks in the world form eighteen separate families, whose members have similar or related characteristics. The largest family is *Carcharhinidae*, whose sixty species are all classed as Requiem sharks, a catch-all term to designate any large, potentially dangerous shark whose man-eating tendencies have frequently led to the celebration of Requiem masses for the dead. A brief look at some of the members of this group will give you an idea of the kinds of sharks that have earned the reputation of being convicted or suspected man-eaters.

GREAT WHITE SHARK

(*Carcharodon carcharias*. Also known as the white shark, man-eater, white death, white pointer.)

The great white shark is undoubtedly the most feared and the most fearsome of all sharks. It is the absolute ruler of the seas, unafraid of any creature be it animal or man. This shark grows longer than thirty-six feet and weighs in excess of seven thousand pounds. It will attack on sight and few victims have been fortunate enough to come away from such an encounter in one piece. The great white is a powerful swimmer that frequently travels alone. It has rows of razor-keen, arrowhead-shaped teeth two inches long and often devours its prey intact. In Australia, where the shark is called the white death, the stomach of one specimen contained the entire carcass of a horse,

GREEK WHITE SHARK *Carcharodon carcharias*

DISTINCTIVE CHARACTERS: Flattened caudal peduncle and crescent-shaped tail. The large, triangular, saw-edged teeth and more rearward position of the anal fin (relative to the second dorsal fin) separate the white shark from the porbeagle and the mako.
COLOR: Slaty brown, dull slate blue, leaden gray, or even almost black above, shading to dirty white below; may have a black spot in the axil of the pectoral; the dorsals and caudal darker along rear edges.
MAXIMUM SIZE: 36½ feet. Size at birth: About 50 inches.
RANGE: Widespread in tropical, subtropical, and warm-temperate belts of all the oceans.
REMARKS: Occurs both inshore and offshore. The white shark feeds often on large prey which it devours practically intact, as illustrated by the presence of other sharks (4 to 7 feet), as well as sea lions, seals, sturgeons, and tuna in the stomachs of some specimens. The white shark is credited with numerous attacks on man in tropical and temperate waters the world over and has thus been given the name "man-eater."

which it had apparently gulped down whole while feeding on the floating refuse of a garbage scow. The great white has been responsible for unprovoked attacks on swimmers off all our coasts. In color it may be slaty brown, dull slate blue, leaden gray or even almost black above, shading to dirty white below. It has a crescent-shaped tail. This species was thought to be a pelagic or ocean-going shark that confined its activities to deep water. But specimens netted within a few yards of the Massachusetts' coast indicate that it appears both inshore and offshore throughout the tropical, subtropical and temperate oceans of the world. The great white is unquestionably the most dangerous shark known to man.

TIGER SHARK

(*Galeocerdo cuvieri*. Also known as leopard shark.)

The tiger shark enjoys a reputation as notorious as that of the great white. Experts consider it one of the deadliest sharks a man can

(57)

TIGER SHARK *Galeocerdo cuvieri*

DISTINCTIVE CHARACTERS: A low lateral ridge on each side of the caudal peduncle; the short blunt snout and the distinct notch in the rear margin of the teeth distinguish this shark from all others.
COLOR: Gray or grayish brown, darker above than on sides and belly; small specimens up to about 5 or 6 feet long are marked on back with darker spots, often fusing irregularly into oblique bars on sides and fins. Markings may fade with growth.
MAXIMUM SIZE: 30 feet. Size at birth: About 19 inches.
RANGE: Worldwide in tropical and subtropical seas; not uncommon along New Jersey coasts during warmer months.
REMARKS: Occasionally taken far out at sea but more often in coastal waters. Stomach contents of tiger sharks have included squids, horseshoe crabs, stingrays, sharks, and many other fishes, turtles, birds, sea lions, and a remarkable assortment of such garbage as carrion, lumps of coal, tin cans, boards, and empty sacks.

encounter. It is known to grow to a length of thirty feet and acquire a heavyweight stature at an early age. A thirteen-foot specimen caught in Hawaiian waters weighed 1,200 pounds. Tiger sharks are aptly named for the striped or spotted markings that appear on the flanks of the younger sharks. With age these markings slowly disappear. The shark's overall coloring is gray or grayish brown. Its short, blunt head and the distinct notch on the margin of the teeth distinguish this shark from all others. Tigers are voracious feeders, swallowing anything that drops into the sea whether it is digestible or not. They frequently travel in schools, which makes them particularly hazardous, especially when their competitive instincts excite them into a mass feeding frenzy. Tiger sharks range throughout the tropical and subtropical seas, often patrol the shallow inshore waters along the Florida coasts and have appeared as far north as New Jersey during warmer months.

MAKO SHARK

(*Isurus oxyrinchus*. Also known as the sharp-nosed mackerel shark.)
The ocean-going mako shark is one of the swiftest swimmers of the shark family. Its maximum size is twelve feet; its average weight

MAKO *Isurus oxyrinchus*

DISTINCTIVE CHARACTERS: Flattened caudal peduncle and crescent-shaped tail. The mako is separable from both the porbeagle and the white shark by its teeth and more slender form; also by the relative position of the second dorsal and anal fins.
COLOR: Deep blue-gray above when fresh caught, but appearing cobalt or ultramarine blue in the water; snow-white below; dirty gray on the lower surface of the pectoral fins.
MAXIMUM SIZE: 12 feet. Size at birth: Unknown.
RANGE: An oceanic species of the tropical and warm-temperate Atlantic; Gulf of Maine to Brazil.
REMARKS: Strong-swimming, pelagic shark, known to leap from the water under natural conditions and when hooked. It is a fisheater, preying upon schools of mackerel, herring, and squid. It is considered to be the only natural enemy of the broadbill swordfish.

is over one thousand pounds. The mako is considered a dangerous shark as well as a supreme fighter on rod and reel. It feeds on mackerel close to the surface and is the only natural enemy of the broadbill swordfish. The mako has a sharply pointed snout and is distinguished by its near symmetrical crescent-shaped tail and the rows of sharp, slender, crooked teeth that often protrude from its jaws. In coloration it ranges from cobalt blue above to a snow-white below. This shark is a tremendous leaper and has been known to jump as high as a cabin cruiser while being fought on hook and line. The mako is found in the tropical and warm-temperate Atlantic, from the Gulf of Maine to Brazil. A closely related species of mako appears in Australia, New Zealand, South Africa and the Indo-Pacific, where it is called the blue pointer.

WHITE-TIPPED SHARK

(*Pterolamiops longimanus*)

Little is known about this ocean-roving shark since it is a true pelagic often seen at sea but seldom seen along coasts. This shark is

WHITE-TIPPED SHARK *Pterolamiops longimanus*

DISTINCTIVE CHARACTERS: Set apart from similar species by the broadly rounded first dorsal fin, short snout, white-tipped fins, and rear tip of the anal fin reaching nearly to the lower precaudal pit.

COLOR: Varying from grayish brown to light gray or pale brown above, and yellowish or dirty white below. In adults the dorsal and pectoral fins are often, but not always, white-tipped. Black-tipped fins are reported on embryos and young specimens.

MAXIMUM SIZE: 12 to 13 feet. Size at birth: About 27 inches.

RANGE: Tropical and subtropical Atlantic, occasionally to Cape Cod.

REMARKS: A pelagic species usually found near the surface in offshore waters where the depth exceeds 100 fathoms. Its diet includes squids, dolphin, mackerels, other small schooling fishes, and garbage.

believed to be responsible for attacks upon survivors of air and sea disasters. It grows to a maximum of twelve or thirteen feet in length and its gray or grayish brown body shading to a white underside is distinctly marked by white-tipped fins. This species ranges far out at sea in the tropical and subtropical parts of the western Atlantic and the eastern Pacific. It is known from Long Island, New York, to Barbados, West Indies, and throughout the Gulf of Mexico.

BAY SHARK

(*Carcharhinus lamiella*)

This shark grows to twelve or fifteen feet in length and is a potentially dangerous species that frequents bays and inshore waters along our western coast. It is common in San Diego Bay and ranges as far south as the central west coast of Mexico. The bay shark closely resembles the bronze whaler of Australia, which is golden bronze in color and has a bad reputation, having been involved in numerous attacks against man.

WHALER SHARK

(Carcharhinus macrurus)

Several species of these sharks are called whalers in Australia and New Zealand because they often prey upon whales in these areas. The whaler sharks have been involved in numerous attacks after which parts of the victims have been found in the sharks' stomachs. The black whaler of Australia attains a length of twelve feet and a weight of almost nine hundred pounds. Other species include the bronze whaler, the brown whaler and the Swan River whaler, which has the added distinction of frequently swimming up fresh-water rivers. The bronze whalers are killer sharks that have definitely been identified in attacks upon human beings.

GREAT BLUE SHARK

(Prionae glauca. Also known as blue shark, blue pointer, blue whaler.)

The great blue shark is probably the most abundant large species of shark found in the Atlantic and Pacific oceans. It attains a length of fifteen to twenty feet and is easily identified by its large pectoral fins, trim stiletto shape and the bright cobalt blue coloration of its back that shades to a snow-white underbelly. This is an open-ocean shark that rarely feeds close to shore. But at sea thousands of them have been sighted schooling together in relatively small areas. They are vicious sharks long believed responsible for old seafaring yarns about sharks following sailing ships for days prior to a death or disaster at sea. It was the blue shark that menaced many survivors of wartime ship sinkings and plane crashes at sea. Men on whaling expeditions often witnessed the ferocity of these sharks swarming to attack captured whales. The species is commonly found offshore but it occasionally comes into shallow water along our North American Pacific Coast. In the western Atlantic ocean it confines its activities mainly to northern waters. But the great blue ranges far and wide throughout all temperate and tropical seas.

(61)

GREAT BLUE SHARK *Prionae glauca*

DISTINCTIVE CHARACTERS: Distinguished from other western Atlantic sharks by the combination of a long pointed snout, a long sickle-shaped pectoral fin, and its blue color.
COLOR: Blue on upper surface, shading to pure white below.
MAXIMUM SIZE: 12 feet 7 inches. Size at birth: About 21 inches.
RANGE: Worldwide in tropical and temperate seas; common along the northeastern United States during warmer months.
REMARKS: Reputedly the most numerous of the large oceanic sharks; it is the one with which sperm whalers were most familiar, and the one around which many superstitions about sharks have developed. Its diet includes herring, mackerel, other small fishes, squid, and garbage.

GREAT HAMMERHEAD SHARKS

(*Sphyrna molarran:* great hammerhead; *Sphyrna lewini:* scalloped hammerhead; *Sphyrna zygaena:* smooth hammerhead; *Sphyrna tiburo:* bonnethead, also known as shovelhead shark.)

Once he has seen it, no one will ever mistake a hammerhead shark for any other species. It is recognized immediately by the strange T-shape of its head, which in all three species except the bonnethead shark resembles the head of a hammer. The smallest and least dangerous member of the family, the bonnethead, has a shovel- (not hammer-) shaped head. Science does not know why these sharks have such a weird head form, but experts speculate that the wing-like lobes may help the species dive or maneuver, much in the manner of diving vanes on submarines. Whether or not this is the reason, the abnormal shape gives the species a particularly formidable appearance, especially since the shark's eyes and nostrils are located at the end of the projecting lobes.

GREAT HAMMERHEAD *Sphyrna molarran*

DISTINCTIVE CHARACTERS: Head indented at midline as in *Sphyrna lewini*, but the corners of the mouth are about opposite the rear margin of the head; both upper and lower teeth are serrated (saw-edged).

COLOR: Small specimens brownish gray above and paler below. The dorsals, both caudal lobes, and upper surfaces of the pectorals are dusky toward the tips. Larger specimens dark olive above and pale olive below.

MAXIMUM SIZE: 15 feet. Size at birth: About 28 inches.

RANGE: Possibly worldwide in tropical and subtropical seas. Details of distribution in Atlantic unknown; reported as far north as North Carolina.

REMARKS: Most specimens recorded offshore. Nothing is known of its diet.

The largest member of the family is the great hammerhead shark, which grows to a length of fifteen feet. Except for the six-foot bonnethead, the maximum lengths of the other species are only slightly less than that of their big brother. The color of these sharks ranges from brownish gray or dark olive above to somewhat paler shades below. They are all dangerous sharks, convicted of occasionally attacking man. In 1959 hammerheads were responsible for at least two attacks. In other instances human remains have been found in their stomachs. Apparently, however, they are not bonafide "attack-on-sight man-eaters" or there would be more fatalities attributed to them, for hammerheads are found not only far at sea but also share the same shallow inshore waters with thousands of bathers. Their reluctance to sample humans more often is obviously not due to a lack of opportunity. But as is true of all sharks possessing the power, capability and sometimes the inclination to attack, the possibility is always present.

Hammerheads are found throughout the world from the tropical and warm-temperate Atlantic to the Gulf of Mexico; the west coast of Central America; from Hawaii to Australia and Indo-China as well as along the coast of India and in the Gulf of Arabia.

LEMON SHARK

(Negaprion brevirostris)

The lemon shark is identifiable by its yellowish-brown coloration and the fact that its dorsal fins are almost the same size. This shark grows to about eleven feet and spends most of its time feeding in shallow coastal waters. The species has often been implicated but never convicted of attacks on humans. But its vicious habits in captivity and the abundant numbers that spend most of their time in shallow water make it a potential danger to swimmers. Lemon sharks are plentiful along Florida coasts and the Caribbean. They have also been reported regularly from Brazil to North Carolina, with strays visiting New Jersey, as well as off the coasts of tropical West Africa and Ecuador.

LEMON SHARK *Negaprion brevirostris*

DISTINCTIVE CHARACTERS: Both dorsal fins triangular and of nearly the same size; distinguished from the sand shark by its blunt snout and by the position and shape of its anal fin, and from the smooth dogfish by its sharp teeth.
COLOR: Yellowish brown to bluish gray above; white to yellowish below.
MAXIMUM SIZE: About 11 feet. Size at birth: About 25 inches.
RANGE: Occurs regularly from Brazil to North Carolina and as a stray to New Jersey.
REMARKS: The diet of this inshore species is not well known; it probably feeds on skates, rays, and a variety of small fishes.

BULL SHARK

(*Carcharhinus leucas*. Also known as cub shark, ground shark, Requiem shark.)

The bull shark differs from other species in having a broadly rounded snout, which tends to give it a bull-headed appearance. It attains a length of twelve feet and will weigh in excess of four hundred pounds at maturity. Its color is gray above and white below; the tips of its pectoral fins are sometimes dusky. This shark is a pelagic species that spends much of its time feeding close to shore and wandering far inland via whatever bays or rivers are available. It has been caught in Louisiana's Atchafalaya River 160 miles from the Gulf. Other reports have placed it at even greater distances up fresh-water tributaries in various parts of the world. This shark's fresh-water cousin is the much feared Lake Nicaragua shark (*Carcharhinus nicaguensis*), which some scientists now believe might migrate back and forth between the Caribbean and Lake Nicaragua.

BULL SHARK (CUB SHARK) *Carcharhinus leucas*

DISTINCTIVE CHARACTERS: Lack of ridge along back between dorsal fins separates this from similar species on the preceding page. Absence of black-tipped fins and a snout which is broadly rounded and shorter than the distance between the nostrils separate the bull shark from the blacktip.
COLOR: Gray above and white below; lower tips of pectorals sometimes dusky.
MAXIMUM SIZE: 12 feet. Size at birth: 28 inches.
RANGE: Common in tropic waters, strays to Long Island.
REMARKS: A sluggish heavy-bodied inshore species, known to enter estuaries and travel up rivers. Feeds on various fishes, other sharks, and garbage.

At least part of this population, however, is thought to have adapted itself entirely to life in fresh water. Only future migratory studies will determine whether this is true.

In some parts of the Gulf of Mexico the bull shark is called the Requiem shark for its reputation as a killer. It is considered one of Florida's most common and most dangerous inshore species. There is speculation that bull sharks may gather along Florida's coasts during certain times of the year for mating purposes. At these times their dispositions may not be as stable as one might wish. Broken tooth fragments left in its victims have implicated this shark in recent attacks. In captivity this species is known to become extremely vicious; yet in their natural environment they do not habitually display their potentially ferocious characters. Bull sharks range from the waters off Cape Hatteras down our eastern Atlantic seaboard, the Bahama Islands, throughout the Caribbean and on down the coast of South America to southern Brazil.

SMALL BLACK-TIPPED SHARK

(*Carcharhinus limbatus*. Also known as black-tip shark, spinner shark, spot-fin shark, carconetta.)

The black-tipped shark is not a large species; it rarely grows to seven or eight feet in length. Its color is gray or ashy blue with a white or yellowish-white underside. Its main identifying characteristic is the black tips of all its fins. This shark is a favorite with light-tackle anglers because of its acrobatic tendencies. Like its big brother, the large black-tipped shark, once hooked it frequently leaps and spins in midair in an attempt to escape. And also like its relative, this shark is considered dangerous, for it has been identified as an occasional attacker. Black-tips are common in tropical and subtropical seas. In the western Atlantic they range as far north as New York and southern New England, down the coast through the Gulf of Mexico and as far south as Brazil. In the eastern Pacific it is found from Baja California to Peru. Reports of this or a similar species have come from as far away as India, China, and the Red Sea.

SMALL BLACK-TIPPED SHARK *Carcharhinus limbatus*

DISTINCTIVE CHARACTERS: Lack of ridge along back between dorsal fins; fins conspicuously tipped with black; differs from the bull shark by its longer snout, and from the large Black-tipped shark by its larger eyes (horizontal diameter ⅓ the length of first gill opening) and more forward position of its first dorsal fin.

COLOR: Gray or ashy blue above, pure white or whitish below; sides with a light wedge-shaped band beginning near the pectoral fins and gradually widening rearward to the pelvic fins where it merges with the white on the belly.

MAXIMUM SIZE: 8 feet. Size at birth: 23 to 26 inches.

RANGE: Southern New England to Brazil, occurring as a stray north of Cape Hatteras, N.C.

REMARKS: An active, swift-swimming shark often seen in schools at the surface. It has a habit of leaping from the water and spiraling through the air before falling back into the sea. Feeds on squid, butterfish, menhaden, and other fishes.

LARGE BLACK-TIPPED SHARK

(Carcharhinus maculipinnis)

The large black-tipped shark differs from the small black-tipped shark in that it grows to eight feet in length, has a slightly longer snout, smaller eyes and a more rearward positioning of its first dorsal fin in relation to its pectoral fin. Otherwise it has the same coloration and habits as the small black-tip. In 1944 this species was identified as the attacker of a fifteen-year-old girl in waist-deep water off Mayport, Florida, near Jacksonville. Packs of these sharks follow coastal-working shrimpboats trawling in that area. They feed voraciously on whatever they can plunder from the nets or whatever trash fish is shoveled overboard. Anglers and shrimp fishermen alike have seen hundreds of black-tips churning the water to a froth during

LARGE BLACK-TIPPED SHARK *Carcharhinus maculipinnis*

DISTINCTIVE CHARACTERS: Lacks ridge on back between dorsal fins; fins conspicuously tipped with black; differs from the bull shark (above) by its longer snout, and from the blacktip by its smaller eyes (horizontal diameter ¼ the length of first gill opening) and more rearward position of the first dorsal relative to the pectorals.
COLOR: Similiar to that of the blacktip shark.
MAXIMUM SIZE: 8 feet. Size at birth: Unknown.
RANGE: Tropical and subtropical western Atlantic; may stray north of Cape Hatteras.
REMARKS: Has the same jumping and spinning habit as the blacktip shark. Little known of its life history and food habits. Probably feeds on squids and small fishes.

these feeding frenzies. It is highly doubtful that anyone falling overboard at such times could avoid being attacked by these sharks. Despite the fact that on rare occasions black-tipped sharks have bitten a wader or swimmer for no apparent reason, under normal circumstances the species is not prone to attack.

SAND SHARK

(*Carcharias taurus*. Also known as sand tiger, Spanish shark.)
Biologists have found that no less than a dozen different species of small coastal-roving sharks have been indiscriminately named sand sharks by laymen who are uncertain of a shark's identity. But there is only one sand shark and it grows over ten feet long with a weight in excess of four hundred pounds. Like the lemon shark this species has dorsal fins of almost equal size, but the difference lies in its more pointed snout, slender, sharply pointed teeth, large, well-developed caudal fin and its markings. Sand sharks are yellowish-brown shading to grayish-white below. Their flanks and caudal fins are marked with

SAND SHARK *Carcharias taurus*

DISTINCTIVE CHARACTERS: Both dorsal fins triangular and of nearly the same size as in the lemon shark and in the smooth dogfish; easily distinguished from the lemon shark by its more pointed snout, and from the smooth dogfish by its sharp pointed teeth and more rearward position of the first dorsal fin.

COLOR: Gray-brown above becoming grayish white below; in some specimens darker spots cover the posterior section of the trunk.

MAXIMUM SIZE: 10 feet 5 inches. Size at birth: About 36 inches.

RANGE: Gulf of Maine to Florida.

REMARKS: One of our most common large sharks during the summer months. The diet of this inshore species includes black drum, bluefish, butterfish, eels, flatfishes, menhaden, and others; reported to travel in schools and surround other fishes.

darker spots of various sizes. During summer months this species is abundant off our northeastern Atlantic coast, and seems to be a year-round resident along the Florida east coast. There has been at least one verified attack by a sand shark in Long Island Sound. In this country the species range from the Gulf of Maine to Florida. They are also common as far south as Brazil, have been reported in the eastern Atlantic, off West and South Africa and in the Mediterranean.

PORBEAGLE SHARK

(*Lamna nasus*. Also known as mackerel shark, blue shark, mako shark.)

If ever a shark had aliases that have confused it with other species, it is the porbeagle, which is often and erroneously called a mako or blue shark. This species' scientific name—*Lamna*—derives from a Greek word meaning "man-eating monster," which gives some idea of how well it was thought of by those who named it. Despite its name and reputation in other parts of the world as being a good shark to avoid, the porbeagle has not as yet been known to attack

(69)

PORBEAGLE (MACKEREL SHARK) *Lamna nasus*

DISTINCTIVE CHARACTERS: Flattened caudal peduncle and crescent-shaped tail. Easily separable from the mako and the white shark by its teeth and by the presence of 2 keels on the caudal fin.
COLOR: Dark bluish gray above, changing abruptly on the lower sides to white; pectoral fins are dusky on outer half or third, the anal fin white or slightly dusky.
MAXIMUM SIZE: 12 feet. Size at birth: About 29 inches.
RANGE: Northern Atlantic, perhaps as far south as South Carolina.
REMARKS: Found inshore as well as offshore, but more abundant in deeper water (40 to 70 fathoms). The porbeagle preys largely on schools of mackerel, herring, and pilchards, following their migrations; also on such goundfish as cod, hake, cusk, flounders, and squid.

man in American waters. Yet this shark, which grows to twelve feet in length and attains a weight of several hundred pounds, has all the potentials. It is a swift-swimming, powerful shark that makes a habit of following and feeding upon schools of mackerel. The porbeagle is a heavy-bodied shark closely resembling the mako and white shark. But unlike the white it has a sharply pointed snout and sharp cusps on the base of its slender, pointed teeth. Its coloration is blue-gray to blackish above with white underside. The porbeagle ranges throughout the north Atlantic and may be found as far south as North Carolina. It is common in the Gulf of Maine, where it is called the blue shark. Across the Atlantic it has been reported from the North Sea to South Africa.

GANGES SHARK

(*Carcharia gangeticus*)

There is no way of knowing how many victims have fallen prey to this voracious river shark named for the Ganges River in India, where it annually takes a terrible toll of lives. The species closely resembles our sand shark (*Carcharia taurus*) and the dreaded gray nurse (*Carcharias arenarius*) of Australia. It ranges throughout the tributaries along the Indian Ocean and is believed to visit Japan also. But its favorite hunting grounds seem to be the murky Ganges River, where it attacks not only Indian pilgrims bathing in that sacred river but also devours corpses consigned to the sanctified waters for burial. McCormick, Allen and Young, in their book *Shadows in the Sea*, mention that these sharks have struck down as many as twenty river bathers in a single year along the Ganges; and that during a two-month period in 1959 sharks killed five persons and mauled thirty others near the mouth of India's Devi River. Little is known about the Ganges River species, but wherever it is encountered it leaves tales of deaths and mutilations in its wake.

NURSE SHARK

(Ginglymostoma cirratum)

This is perhaps one of the laziest species of the entire shark family. It inhabits the shallows, frequently in water only a few feet deep, where it lethargically lies in wait for whatever fish or squid may come its way. This is one of the shark species that need not swim in order to breathe, for it is capable of pumping water through its gill clefts while lying motionless. Because it rests frequently on the bottom, lacks the aggressive appearance of other sharks and does not have the dagger-like teeth of the more vigorous members of the clan, the nurse shark makes a tempting target for skindivers. But appearances are deceiving. The Atlantic nurse shark is considered dangerous because it is often short-tempered and resents being tampered with. Its sluggish disposition sometimes invites investigations by curious or playful swimmers. But this frequently results in prompt retaliation by the shark. A typical attack by a nurse shark occurred off Miami Beach in 1958 when a skindiver grabbed hold of the shark's tail in the hopes of getting a free ride. Instead of the ride, he got bitten on the thigh by the five-foot shark, which held on tenaciously until the diver reached his boat. And then it took ten minutes to pry the shark's jaws loose from the boy's leg. These instances are common, and most have been provoked by the victim.

NURSE SHARK *Ginglymostoma cirratum*

DISTINCTIVE CHARACTERS: Set apart from all other sharks of the western Atlantic by the long barbel on the margin of each nostril and the deep groove connecting the nostril with the mouth.

COLOR: Yellowish to grayish brown, darker above than below. Small specimens may have dark spots on body or brown crossbars on the fins; adults may or may not retain these markings.

MAXIMUM SIZE: 14 feet. Size at birth: About 11 inches.

RANGE: Common in Caribbean and southern Florida with migrations to North Carolina. Occurs as stray to Rhode Island.

REMARKS: Appears chiefly inshore, often in water as shallow as 2 to 10 feet. Sometimes travels in schools and feeds mainly on shrimps, squids, crabs, and small fishes.

Nurse sharks grow to a maximum of fourteen feet in length and are the only species with long, drooping barbels or "whiskers" protruding from the nostrils. They are yellowish to grayish-brown above, shading to a lighter underside. Nurse sharks are common throughout the Caribbean and southern Florida waters, occurring as a stray to Rhode Island. Although they have the same common name as the nurse shark of Australia, the two species are completely different.

All the sharks mentioned in the foregoing part of this chapter are known or suspected of being dangerous to man. The two that follow are just the opposite.

WHALE SHARK

(*Rhincodon typus*)

The whale shark is the largest fish in the world, and one of the most harmless. This gigantic creature is similar to the whale in size

WHALE SHARK *Rhincodon typus*

DISTINCTIVE CHARACTERS: Unique because of its great size and spotted color pattern; its mouth is at tip of snout; prominent ridges on the sides of the body.
COLOR: Dark gray to reddish or greenish brown on sides; marked with round white or yellow spots and a number of white or yellow transverse bars; white or yellow below.
MAXIMUM SIZE: 45 feet. Size at birth: Unknown.
RANGE: All tropical oceans; reported as far north as Long Island.
REMARKS: This offshore species is the largest living fish known to man. It does not bear its young alive, but deposits egg capsules. Its diet is composed mainly of plankton and small fishes.

only, for it is all shark, up to forty-five feet long, and there is reason to believe that some may grow to seventy-five feet. A thirty-eight-foot specimen caught off Knight's Key, Florida, weighed 26,594 pounds. A single egg case of this species is over two feet long and a foot wide. The diet of this enormous creature consists exclusively of tiny marine organisms and small fish, which it catches by rushing through the ocean with its cavernous mouth open. The water surges in and escapes through its gill rakers, which filter out the millions of microscopic plankton organisms that serve as the whale shark's food. This species is easily recognized by its immense size and spotted coloration. The body is dark gray to reddish or greenish brown above and on its sides, marked with round white or yellow spots and a number of white or yellow transverse bars. Its underside is white or yellow. Perhaps because of their size, whale sharks do not frighten easily. There are numerous instances on record of boats pulling alongside this fish and men climbing onto the shark's back to examine it as the creature swam slowly along the surface. Whale sharks are found in all tropical oceans and have been reported as far north as Long Island.

BASKING SHARK

(*Centorhinus maximus*. Also known as the bone shark, sailfish shark, elephant shark, sunfish.)

The basking shark is exceeded in size only by the whale shark. It grows to a length of forty-five feet and possibly more. This sluggish species presents more of a shark-like appearance than does the whale shark. With its pointed snout and sleeker body lines, it somewhat resembles an enlarged version of the mako shark. But this great shark is harmless, if any creature weighing as much as two elephants can be considered harmless. Like the whale shark, it feeds only on small fish and marine plankton, which it filters from the water with the sieve-like combs of its enormous gill rakers. Basking sharks are slaty gray or black above, shading to a lighter color below. As their name suggests, these sharks spend much of their time basking on the surface. Since they often travel in large schools and sometimes

BASKING SHARK *Cetorhinus maximus*

DISTINCTIVE CHARACTERS: The combination of a crescent-shaped tail, enormously long gill openings, long gill rakers, and numerous minute teeth sets the basking shark apart from all others.
COLOR: Grayish brown to slaty gray or nearly black above; underside may be same color or lighter than the back, sometimes with a triangular white patch under the snout and two pale bands on the belly.
MAXIMUM SIZE: 45 feet. Size at birth: 5 to 6 feet.
RANGE: Has been reported in the Gulf of Maine and off northeastern shores. Only one report farther south than North Carolina. In the past, there have been numerous reports of basking sharks off Massachusetts and on occasion off New York and New Jersey.
REMARKS: Basking sharks often gather in schools and swim sluggishly near the surface. In the winter it is assumed they retire to deeper water. Their diet consists of plankton which they sift out of the water by means of their gill rakers.

have the peculiar habit of swimming nose-to-tail with other basking sharks, this has given rise to many sea-serpent stories. Imagine a file of five or six forty-foot basking sharks cruising the surface one behind the other with their backs, dorsals and tails exposed. Visualize how that sight would look at a distance and you will understand why some people thought they were witnessing a two hundred-foot sea serpent! And the myth does not stop there. Many sea-monster stories can be traced to the skeletons of basking sharks washed up on beaches. With its enormous jaws and gill arches, its long, tapering vertebral column and its "leg-like" fin supports, the peculiar sight has stirred many an imaginative mind with visions of sea serpents.

In the past basking sharks were hunted for the oil in their livers. A single shark could produce eighty to six hundred gallons of oil. But with the development of petroleum, hunting the basking shark became commercially unfeasible. Today this pelagic species roams free in vast numbers from temperate to northern seas, south to Iceland and along the coasts of Norway, Scotland and Ireland. On our northeastern Atlantic coast strays appear in the Gulf of Maine. They have also been sighted along the Pacific coast near Monterey and San Simeon bays, California, as well as off Peru, Ecuador, Australia, China and Japan.

6

Fighting the Menace

Few men have ever been attacked by the most feared man-eater of all—the great white shark—and lived to tell about it. Australian skin-diver Rodney Fox is one who did.

It was a sparkling clear Sunday morning in December 1963. Fox had joined forty other divers on Aldinga Beach to compete in the annual South Australian Skindiving and Spearfishing Championship. The event was to last five hours. Using no artificial breathing aids, competitors would "free-dive" along the inshore reef and acquire points by the variety and weights of the fish they speared. Fox had won the 1961–62 championship, had been a runner-up the following season and was anxious to win the title this year. He was an adept diver and a good spearfisherman. He had trained himself to dive safely to one hundred feet and hold his breath for more than a minute without discomfort. As the nine o'clock whistle blast announced the opening of the competition he waded into the surf.

On a long line attached to his weight belt each man towed a large, hollow fish float. These floats were to hold the speared fish to prevent blood getting into the water and attracting sharks. As an added precaution two high-powered speedboats patroled the area.

Fox found good hunting on the reef. By noon he had brought ashore sixty pounds of fish. The contest was to end in two hours. On his last swim-in from a section of the reef that dropped off abruptly from twenty-five- to sixty-foot depths, he had seen a large fish resting near a triangular rock. That fish, plus one more of another species, could cinch the title for him.

When he returned to the spot the fish was still there. Cautiously he dove down and glided toward it, aiming his speargun at the twenty-pound prize, hopeful of making a clean, close-in kill.

Suddenly a perceptible hush fell over the reef. Everything seemed poised, motionless. Then something struck Fox a tremendous blow on his left side, knocking him sideways. The next thing he knew he was being pushed through the water in a blur of speed. His mask and speargun were ripped away. His back and chest felt as if they were being crushed; his insides squeezed over against his right side. The pressure on his body seemed to be choking him, still he did not know what was happening. He tried to squirm free but found himself clamped in a vise-like grip. Then, with horrible clarity, he realized that a shark had him in its jaws.

"I couldn't see the creature, but it had to be a huge one," said Fox later. "Its teeth had closed around my chest and back, with my left shoulder forced into its throat. I was being thrust face down ahead of it as we raced through the water."

Although dazed and shocked, Fox felt no pain. Only the terrible pressure on his body. He stretched his arms out behind, groping for the shark's head, trying to gouge its eyes.

Suddenly the pressure disappeared as the shark relaxed its jaws. Fox thrust backward to push himself away—but his right arm went straight into the monster's mouth. Now he felt pain the likes of which he had never imagined. Blinding bursts shot through every part of his body. As he wrenched his arm loose from the jagged teeth waves of agony swept over him. But at least he was free.

Blindly he thrashed and kicked his way to the surface, repeatedly colliding with the shark's body. Frantically he gulped air and shouted an alarm. He knew the shark would come up for him. A fin brushed his flippers, then rough hide scraped his knees. In a wild effort to avoid its hideous jaws Fox grabbed at the shark and clamped his legs around the enormous body.

Down he went again, clinging to the shark until he scraped rocks on the bottom. Then he pushed away with all his remaining strength. He had to get back to the surface to breathe.

When he reached it the water was crimson with his blood. The shark breached the surface a few feet away, its huge rust-colored body rolling on its side like a giant tree trunk, its gaping jaws and conical head unmistakably those of the most feared of man-eaters—the great white death itself!

It surged toward Fox, and in those brief seconds he knew in utter terror what was about to happen. Then suddenly, miraculously, the shark veered away from him. Fox saw his fish float race across the water. The slack line tightened at his belt and he was pulled forward and under the water again. At the last instant the shark had lunged for the float instead of him and had fouled itself in the line. Fox fumbled to release his weight belt, to which the line was attached, but he was too weak. By now he was moving very fast as he was helplessly dragged under water thirty or forty feet. His lungs were bursting and one thought rushed through his mind: *Surely I'm not going to drown now.*

Then the final miracle occurred: the line parted. Fox was free again. Somehow he managed to get back to the surface. A patrol boat picked him up and he was rushed to a hospital. Those who examined him were appalled by the extent of his injuries. His right hand and arm were so badly slashed that the bones lay bare in several places. His chest, back, left shoulder and side were deeply gashed. Great pieces of flesh had been torn aside, exposing the rib cage, lungs and upper stomach.

Despite his injuries Rodney Fox lived through his ordeal with the white death. There are many that have not.

Australia has always ranked high on shark attack lists. In 1963, Gilbert P. Whitley of the Australian Museum at Sydney, New South Wales, reported that there had been 390 recorded cases of sharks attacking human beings, horses, dogs, boats, or surf-skis in Australian waters; of these about 118 persons were killed. In the last six years this figure has increased. It is always difficult in such cases to correctly identify the species of shark responsible for killing bathers. But from the data available Whitley said it seemed that the whaler sharks of several species were the most deadly, followed by the tiger shark, white shark, gray nurse shark, and perhaps in rare cases, the blue pointer shark (*Isuropsis mako*) and the hammerhead shark. It has been proved that sharks feed during the day or night on the ebb, flow or slack of the tide. Humans have been attacked at various hours, but most commonly between 3 and 6 .P.M. in depths ranging from ankle-deep to open sea, under all kinds of sea and beach conditions. Interestingly, most attacks on Australian bathers occurred in about four feet of water from ten to twenty-five yards offshore. This, of course, does not indicate that sharks are most commonly found in these depths or that they prefer this zone for attack. It indicates only that sharks are not reluctant to enter these depths.

An Australian surgeon, Dr. V. M. Coppleson, made a lifelong study of publicized shark attacks and developed some interesting theories about them, many of which he describes in his book *Shark Attack!* Coppleson believed that many attacks were caused by a "rogue shark." He defined this shark as "a killer which having experienced the deadly sport of killing and mauling a human, goes in search of similar game." Coppleson compared them to man-eating lions and tigers that especially seek out humans for prey.

One dramatic event that seemed to support his rogue shark theory occurred in January 1940. Coppleson had noted that in 1934 in George's River, near Sydney, two persons were attacked about three miles apart within a period of four hours, one of them at almost the exact spot where a man had been attacked less than a year before. Was a rogue shark attack pattern developing for this area? In 1940, when Coppleson read a newspaper account reporting that dogs were being attacked by sharks at George's River, he suspected it was the work of a solitary killer. When a thirteen-year-old boy was killed by a shark at North Brighton Beach, not far from George's River, he became convinced of it. The fatal attack occurred on January 23, 1940. That day Coppleson wrote a letter to the *Sydney Morning Herald* warning that a man-eating shark was in the area and might strike again. Eleven days after his letter was published a man was killed by a shark four hundred yards from the scene of the first attack.

To further substantiate his theory Coppleson relied heavily upon circumstances surrounding a series of attacks that occurred off New Jersey in the early 1900s. On July 1, 1916, Charles Van Sant was killed by a shark at Beach Haven, New Jersey. Six days later Charles Bruder was killed by a shark at Spring Lake, forty-five miles from Beach Haven. On July 12, six days after the Bruder attack, two deaths and a mutilation occurred on the same day at Matawan Creek, New Jersey. Matawan Creek is seventy miles as a shark would swim from where Van Sant was attacked at Beach Haven, and twenty-five miles as a shark would swim from where Bruder was attacked at Spring Lake. Two days after the Matawan Creek attacks a great white shark eight and a half feet long was netted in a bay four miles from the mouth of the creek. Its stomach contained fifteen pounds of human flesh and several bone fragments. This shark may or may not have been the rogue to blame for all five of these July attacks, but it was probably involved in some of them. Coppleson felt that successive attacks could occur along the path of a single shark—a cruising rogue shark—up to distances of sixty to eighty miles. All of the July 1916 New Jersey attacks took place well within this range. But it is also worth noting that authorities considered 1916 a year in which unprecedented numbers of sharks were both seen and killed along the New Jersey coast. It was, as scientific experts of the era called it, an unusually bad "shark year."

If Coppleson's theory is correct, what would cause a shark to become a rogue? No one knows for sure, but in the higher animals—lions and tigers, for example—many become man-eating rogues when age or some physical affliction prevents them from catching fleeter game. Several years ago I witnessed the capture of what could have been a rogue shark. I was fishing with the Florida Shark Club of Jacksonville on a beach near St. Augustine. One of the members, Paul Eastman, caught an eight-foot tiger shark. As we beached the catch we noticed that the tiger was practically all head; its long, sinuous body was badly wasted away. Then we saw why. Tangled tightly around the shark's caudal peduncle, just ahead of its tail, was a trailing fifteen-foot length of yellow nylon anchor rope. The rope had been there long enough to cut through the tough hide and cause a deep, festering wound. Dragging the rope had apparently prevented the shark from swimming fast enough to catch much food, which accounted for its emaciated condition. Examination of the stomach contents revealed that it had been feeding in the surf on slow-moving trash fish, and very few of those. No one can say when this tiger shark might have turned into a rogue and attacked the easiest prey of all—a human being. But one thing is certain—thanks to Paul Eastman that potential threat is no longer roving Florida's beaches.

In 1919 Coppleson collected all the published accounts of shark attacks he could find and began studying them for patterns of similarity, essentially the same thing that scientists are doing now with world-wide Shark Attack Files. Again, allowing for the unpredictability of sharks and exceptions to the rule, Coppleson's findings were remarkably accurate. He noted, for example, that *most* attacks occurred at sea temperatures of 70° F or higher, which scientists were to find is a temperature range in which many species of sharks are most active. It is also the thermal zone in which bathers are most likely to be more numerous. However, in 1959, within three hours after a great white shark killed Albert Kogler in San Francisco Bay, the water temperature was taken at the site of attack. It was 55° F.

Coppleson noted that in Australian waters it was remarkable how many reports referred to sandbanks some distance from shore, separated from the beach by a channel. Many experienced surfers believed this was the formation most likely to attract sharks. In studying attacks on surfers he found that the victims selected from a group of surf riders was often the individual who missed the wave while the others went on. Rarely was the victim plucked from the middle of a throng. Usually it was the lone swimmer or someone separated from a small party who caught the shark's attention.

It was Coppleson's theory that more shark attacks occurred on the east coast of continents than on the west due to the fact that the western shores were usually bound by colder water currents. Attack statistics bore him out. He formulated a world-wide timetable for shark attacks, charting the months and geographical areas in which shark attacks would most likely occur. Again, it proved accurate.

Over the years amateurs and experts alike have proposed many schemes and devices to end shark attacks. These have included mechanical noise-makers to scare sharks away; electrical barriers to shock them away; air-bubble curtains to frighten them away; and hunter-killer task forces of boats and planes to exterminate them. None of these methods has been too successful. The most effective device found for protecting beaches in shark-infested waters is what Australians call "meshing." The technique is to place loosely hanging nets in the water overnight around the bathing beaches. These are designed to entangle sharks and thus reduce the shark population. First tried at Sydney's big beaches in 1937, the nets caught fifteen hundred sharks, nine hundred of them probable man-eaters, in just over a year. Since then the catch has dropped to about two hundred a year, and the number of attacks on bathers at meshed beaches has fallen to zero.

When Durban, South Africa, tried meshing along their beaches results were equally successful. Annual catch records between 1952, when 552 sharks were caught, and 1960, when 117 were caught, indicate a marked decrease in Durban's shark population due to meshing. Wherever the method has been used it has proved effective, but it is limited to relatively small areas. At unmeshed beaches shark attacks continue. And what about the survivors of plane and ship disasters at sea? How do you protect *them* from the threat of shark attack?

This was one of the most fervently asked questions of World War II. It was on the mind of every airman who knew he might have to ditch his plane over shark-infested seas. It was on the mind of every sailor, soldier or merchant marine who knew he might have his ship blasted out from under him. Of all the undersea creatures none was so universally dreaded as the shark. After ship sinkings or aircraft abandonment at sea, when loss of life was expected and accepted, death by shark attack evoked a horror that had no equal among the evils faced on land. When at last the military authorities were confronted with the question, it was after shipwrecked men and downed aviators began to tell their stories of encounters with sharks. And there were thousands of them—some harmless, some grim.

One of the latter is reported in the files of the United States Coast Guard's Search and Rescue Agency. A Navy pilot had to ditch his plane in the central Pacific and was pulled unconscious from the wreckage by his radioman. Floating in their life jackets, they were soon aware of sharks swimming around them. Suddenly the radioman was attacked on his right foot. The pilot later reported:

"I told him to get on my back and keep his right foot out of water, but, before he could, the shark struck again and we were both jerked under water for a second. I knew we were in for it as there were more than five sharks around and blood all around us.

"He showed me his leg and not only did he have bites all over his right leg but his left thigh was badly mauled. He wasn't in any particular pain except every time they struck I knew it and felt the jerk. I finally grabbed my binoculars and started swinging them at the passing sharks.

"It was a matter of seconds when they struck again. . . . His head was under water and his body jerked as the sharks struck it. As I drifted away . . . sharks continually swam about and every now and then I could feel one with my foot. At midnight I sighted a [U.S. patrol] boat and was rescued after calling for help."

Reports such as these indicated that the shark problem required more careful investigation, that the possibility of developing a counter-measure was not only necessary but essential to the war effort. In 1942 scientists began research aimed at finding a chemical shark repellent. By the end of 1942 experiments indicated that copper acetate, when allowed to diffuse slowly in water, would prevent sharks from taking a bait. It was reported to be 95.2 percent effective. When combined with nigrosine dye mixed with Carbowax, it was packaged and distributed to the Armed Forces. Someone named it "Shark Chaser."

In actual use the repellent proved to turn away some species of sharks, particularly individual sharks. But others swam through the dye and even gulped down packets of the repellent. When droves of sharks crazed by blood in the water went on a feeding frenzy, biting chunks out of everything in sight, including other sharks, the repellent was of no practical value. The effectiveness of Shark Chaser lay in the psychological relief it gave those who had it to use. If men *believed* it would repell sharks, then that in itself made it of immeasurable value. With Shark Chaser many were to survive subsequent encounters with sharks when otherwise they might have given up hope.

Although Shark Chaser is still the most effective chemical repellent we have, scientists have conducted many experiments in an effort to either improve it or find something better. In extensive tests on dangerous sharks at Bimini's Lerner Marine Laboratory, Dr. Perry W. Gilbert, chairman of the Shark Research Panel, found that the bluish-black nigrosine dye of Shark Chaser was "possibly more repellent to sharks than is the copper acetate. . . . The value of copper acetate as shark repellent is open to serious question."

Recently, Dr. Sydney Galler, Chief of Naval Research in Biology, announced that the Navy was sponsoring the study of a new type of repellent derived from sea cucumbers. Scientists got the idea when they found that this marine creature protects itself from sharks and other denizens of the deep by ejecting a powerful poison called holothurin, which can send fish into violent convulsions. It was also found that sharks died after being put in tanks occupied a month previously by sea cucumbers.

(83)

Inventor John Hicks is testing an electronic repellent, which, when the device is activated, emits shock-like radio waves that supposedly send sharks fleeing. Trials in the Atlantic reportedly caused large hammerhead sharks to retreat hastily when they came within range of Hick's device. Other tests ended less conclusively. When Dr. Gilbert tried an electrical repellent on dangerous sharks in Bimini it adequately repelled lemon sharks, but tiger sharks were attracted to it and repeatedly returned for more low-voltage jolts of electricity.

Dr. C. Scott Johnson of the Naval Undersea Warfare Center in San Diego, California, has had good results with a "survival sack" he designed called Shark Screen. It consists of a six-foot-long black plastic bag whose open end is encircled by a flotation collar of three air-filled rings colored yellow for visibility. The survival sack would be attached to life jackets and quickly inflated. A survivor would then climb into it and float upright, the bag and contents supposedly appearing to a shark as any other nondescript flotsam drifting on the ocean surface. Johnson's Shark Screen is presently scheduled for further tests with the Navy.

Pending discoveries of more effective means of discouraging shark attacks, the American Institute of Biological Sciences Shark Research Panel offers these safety rules for those who frequent or find themselves in shark-infested waters.

1. ALWAYS SWIM OR DIVE WITH A COMPANION. Most attacks are made on lone swimmers. A companion affords better hope of summoning help or reaching shore if an attack occurs. Also, a companion may be able to improvise a tourniquet or in some other way slow loss of blood from a bad bite.

2. DO NOT SWIM AT NIGHT OR IN VERY MURKY WATER. Sharks are difficult to see at night. In dark or murky water they are more likely to mistake a bather for something edible.

3. DO NOT ENTER OR REMAIN IN WATER WITH AN OPEN CUT. Sharks are attracted by blood. They can smell faint traces of blood even when some distance away. If you are cut while swimming, try to bind the wound and leave the water immediately. Along with this goes special advice to spearfishermen: Do not tow speared fish on your belt. All catches should be boated or taken ashore at once.

4. Do not panic or thrash after sighting a shark. If a shark is sighted, leave the water immediately, but with as little splashing as possible. When swimming, use a steady, even stroke to reach shore or a boat.

5. If a shark moves in, hit it on the snout with any object available, preferably a heavy one. Don't strike a shark with your fist except as a last resort. Rough hide will only cut your skin and make you bleed.

6. Never tease or spear a shark no matter how small or harmless it may seem. Sharks react the way any wild animal reacts once it has been provoked: it bites its attacker.

A cruising shark ignores Dr. C. Scott Johnson who is testing a plastic survival bag he designed called "Shark Screen."

7. DO NOT TRAIL ARMS OR LEGS FROM AN AIR MATTRESS OR LIFE RAFT. Dangling hands, arms or legs may offer a tempting target to feeding sharks. Keep them out of the water to avoid encouraging an attack.

8. IF YOU HAVE CLOTHES ON, DON'T TAKE THEM OFF. They protect you from shark-skin lacerations. Shoes, especially, should be left on.

9. ADOPT A SENSIBLE ATTITUDE TOWARD SHARKS. Remember that the likelihood of attack is less than that of being struck by lightning. Attack is almost assured, however, when one deliberately grabs or otherwise molests any shark.

7

Shark Fishing

At 9 A.M. one morning at Durban, South Africa, a boy wearing swimming trunks and carrying a long Calcutta fishing rod clambered out to the sea end of the seven hundred-yard-long forty-foot-wide jumble of concrete blocks called the South Pier. He baited his big hook with whale liver, whirled the long wire leader overhead and arced it out into the choppy blue waters of the Atlantic Ocean.

A half hour later he had a vicious strike that tore out five hundred yards of his line. Somehow he turned the fish, gained some of his line, then lost it again. This happened repeatedly. Two hours later the boy was *winching*—that is, he was squatted down with the rod butt wedged under his right ankle and the rod braced over his left knee while he used both hands to force crank the reel. Each time the fish lunged forward the boy was hoisted bodily off the pier, teetering on the side of his ankle but remaining wrapped around his rod until the fish turned and dropped him back against the rough concrete. He did this for five hours. In the end he got up, laid the rod over his shoulder and strained like a plow horse in harness away from the fish, gaining line a foot at a time. Somehow he clambered back over the seven hundred yards of concrete blocks to the beach. Finally, the thing he had caught was dragged ashore. It was a 764-pound blue pointer shark, better known in other parts of the world as the great white or man-eater shark. The boy managed a smile of victory, but five hours of scrubbing on the concrete pier had taken its toll on his body. Parts of him looked like freshly ground hamburger.

Across the ocean from him a Jacksonville, Florida, shark fisherman spent three days and nights sleeping on a thirty-inch-wide concrete bridge walk waiting for a shark to take his bait. When it finally did, it took five hundred yards, or $23.50 worth, of the angler's line as well.

On a northwest Florida pier near Panama City an angler hooked a large shark on a reel loaded with steel line usually reserved for deep-sea bottom-fishing. The fish steamed seaward with such determination that the harnessed angler asked bystanders to hold onto him. When it became apparent that the shark had no intention of turning, they advised him to cut the wire and let the thing go. He refused. At line's end the angler was snatched from their grasp, whisked down the pier and catapulted over the railing, breaking the line as he hit the water.

On a Texas pier a determined shark fisherman stood by his rod for twenty-two consecutive nights waiting for a strike. On the twenty-third night he hit the jackpot. He caught two, lost three and the third shark made toothpicks of his rod.

No matter how many miles separated these four fishermen, they all had one thing in common—an acute case of shark fever. You won't find it listed in the medical dictionary and no wonder drugs will cure it. But once you catch it you will be hooked as surely as the shark on the other end of your line.

Shark fever is the fanatical, almost uncontrollable, urge to fight big sharks on hook and line. It is big-game fishing on a shoestring. There may be safer, more spectacular fish to fight, and fancier, more expensive ways to fight them, but few forms of angling provide quite so much difficulty, diabolical unpredictability and dramatic results in one big lump as does the sport of shark fishing. This is why it is rapidly acquiring a growing, wildly enthusiastic following of sportsmen who not so many years ago had overlooked the shark as a sport fish.

Today, shark fishing, the rough, tough, challenging sport of British, South African and Australian anglers, is achieving new heights of popularity among America's salt-water Izaak Waltons. In answer to its growing number of enthusiasts, shark-fishing clubs have mushroomed into existence on every coast from Miami, Florida, to Montauk, Long Island, to Monterey Bay, California. Twice a year at Moss Landing, sixty miles south of San Francisco, scores of sportsmen and spectators gather for a shark-fishing derby. In the course of the six-hour event some two thousand pounds of sharks and rays are fought and landed. Across the country, the Palm Beach Sharkers in one six-month period caught twenty-one sharks that averaged 318 pounds apiece from a pier near the world's famous bathing beach. At Boynton Beach Inlet to the north, Herb Goodman, the seventy-year-old "One-Man Shark Club" of Lake Worth, Florida, fought and landed his 160th shark of over six feet long. At Nassau Sound, near Little Talbot Island, hundreds of holiday spectators turned out to watch the day-and-night "sharkathons" of the Florida Shark Club of Jacksonville, whose fifty members battle sharks from beaches, boats and piers to eliminate annually more than two hundred of the large predators. And this is only a sampling.

A survey by the U. S. Fish and Wildlife Service estimated that sport fishermen in this country are catching 1,715,000 sharks a year and 45 percent of these are being taken between Maine and North Carolina alone. Typical of the growth of the sport is the history of a shark tournament held annually at Bay Shore, Long Island. There were six boats participating in the event when it began in 1960. During last summer's tourney more than two hundred boats put to sea. Several years ago the Sandy Hook Marine Laboratory in New Jersey launched a shark-tagging program. It now receives approximately four hundred letters a season from prospective shark anglers. When the U. S. Government Printing Office published a 25¢ booklet titled "The Anglers' Guide to Sharks" (Circular 179) in response to this interest, it surprised everyone by becoming an overnight best seller. There were 22,446 copies of this publication printed for sale and 22,131 have been sold. It is presently in its fifth reprinting.

Why this attraction to sharks? At best, the only reward a shark hunter gets is a tough, torturous, muscle-straining fight that leaves him completely worn out. There are probably as many reasons for a man to volunteer for this kind of punishment as there are individual shark fishermen. But basically it is the challenge, the desire to take on the indisputable sovereign of the seas and try to best him. "When you get a ten-footer full of fight you have something on your hands," said Bing Shows, past president of the Florida Shark Club of Jacksonville. "I've fought sharks as long as three hours, and then I couldn't move for days."

Without exception, sharks are the only deep-sea giants that have

Bing Shows rests momentarily during a fight with a shark at sea. The angler's shoulder harness prevents the big reel from wobbling and lets him absorb some of the strain with his back. Meatgrinder in foreground is used to grind chum (bait fish) to entice sharks.

no qualms about entering and feeding in the shallow coastal waters. This means that they are readily available to any adequately equipped angler with the stamina and determination to fight them. It is an unsurpassed opportunity for a taste of big-game fishing at a fraction of the cost for a single day's trip aboard a charter boat. Man may not have learned how to curb the shark's predacious, often fatal attacks on humans yet, but what he has learned is that this fish, which has been shrouded in mystery and myth, may also be the world's best game fish.

On a line the deadly fighters have displayed such star-studded performances that the International Game Fish Association lists six species of sharks on their honor roll of forty-eight big-game fish. Top fighter of the lot is the mako shark, which weighs over one thousand pounds and which many big-game fishermen consider the ultimate game fish. A mako will repeatedly hurl its massive body ten to fifteen feet into the air, whirling on its axis to wrap line and leader about itself in an effort to escape. Some have literally rocketed into the cockpit of a cabin cruiser, dispersing anglers and taking part of the transom with them when they left. The same is true of the great white or man-eater shark, which for years has topped the IGFA's

This 11-foot 1,060-pound Great White shark was a prize catch for scientists at Florida's Mote Marine Laboratory. It was caught on a long-line off Midnight Pass near Sarasota.

list of biggest game fish caught on rod and reel. It is a 2,644-pounder taken by Alfred Dean off Cedua, Australia, in 1959. In 1964 famous Montauk shark-fishing charter-boat captain Frank Mundus, who takes devotees "monster fishing" aboard his boat *Cricket* II, harpooned a 4,500-pound great white. Mundus specializes in letting his customers fight ricocheting makos on light tackle, an experience guaranteed to bring them back for more.

Not all sharks can be classified in the same fighting category as makos and man-eaters. Some strike fast and savagely; others are slow starters and mulish fighters. On light tackle a black-tip or a spinner shark possess similar characteristics of the mako, with its constant jumping and spinning maneuvers, while the nurse shark simply bulldozes along. But between these two extremes are the porbeagle, blue, lemon, thresher, bull, silky and tiger sharks. And what they have to offer the sportsman is considerable. Despite what many anglers of fancier fish care to admit, the sheer brute power behind most sharks is formidable. When biologist Stewart Springer used a device called a dynamometer to measure the pull of different sharks caught while shark fishing, the record was impressive. Springer found that a ten-foot hammerhead, without a run, could exert an initial pull of fifteen

Small sharks are good sport on light tackle. Miles of shallow sand flats in the Florida keys abound with these gamesters.

hundred pounds. An adult silky shark—a species weighing not more than 350 pounds—could, if permitted a twenty-yard run, always break a snubbed manila rope whose minimum breaking strength was approximately 1,350 pounds. Great white sharks were able to break wire rope or chain having a breaking strength of 3,800 pounds! It is strength such as this that challenges shark fishermen to best these tackle-busters on fishing lines that break at pressures over eighty or 130 pounds.

Not all sharks are giants, therefore they have been caught on all manner of tackle ranging from fly rods to the volleyball big-game reels and rods. Normal salt-water spinning reels loaded with twenty-pound-test monofilament, a fifteen-foot wire leader and a 9/0 to 12/0 hook, are capable of handling sharks up to 150 pounds. Heavier fish demand heavier tackle, and the favorite sporting combination is a 9/0 reel spooled with five hundred yards of eighty-pound-test dacron. Since sharks can reach beyond normal-length leaders and cut the line with one slice of their tails, leaders on the heavier rigs are frequently twenty to thirty feet of flexible outboard-motor tiller cable. Boat rods are about six feet long, fairly stiff and made of fiberglass. Beach and pier rods are often homemade of Calcutta bamboo and range up to fourteen feet in length. A shark hunter can outfit himself with big-game shark-fishing equipment for around $100, or rent gear from local tackle shops whenever it is available. After that all he needs is his bait and a proper place to deploy it. Although sharks are not particular about what kind of meal they are served, the best bait seems to be bonito skewered on one or more of the big hooks. Bonito is a bloody fish that sharks seldom pass up. Menhaden, mullet, amberjack and ray are good second choices.

The surest and simplest way of locating sharks is from a boat. Baits are either dropped to the bottom or fished ten feet below the surface by attaching inflated balloons to the leader. To attract sharks anglers mince bait fish through a meat grinder and throw handfuls of this chum overboard. If sharks are around it won't take them long to find the source of this tantalizing appetizer. Sharkers fishing from shore frequently balloon out their baits on an outgoing tide or use canoes to carry them through the surf and drop them offshore. The sharks are then fought from the beach. Piers, jetties and bridges are excellent launching sites for shark baits.

Once the bait is placed, the reel is put out of gear and on its clicker. Sharks frequently pick up the baits and carry them in their jaws before swallowing, so while line is clicking off the reel, usually at a high-speed, nerve-wracking whine, the angler has to grit his teeth and wait as long as he can stand it before throwing the reel in gear and striking. From then on anything can happen. The reel usually steps up its speed despite the drag of the brake, until it is whirring like a Tibetan prayer wheel and wailing like forty scared banshees. Line streaks through the rod guides in a blur, and two hundred yards or more seems to melt off the spool in a matter of seconds. It is at these times that a shark fisherman appreciates what a good shoulder harness and rod-butt belt can do to take a little of the tremendous pressure off his straining muscles. Sometime in the initial couple of minutes he has to turn the shark, force it into a more oblique run, or; better still, fight it into reversing its ground and swimming back toward him so he can gain some line. At all costs the angler must keep the shark moving, because once stopped, a shark recovers its strength rapidly. The kind of shark, the size of the shark and how much luck is on the side of the angler will determine the outcome of the fight.

Sooner or later the catch will have to be landed. On shore

bystanders will be glad to lend a hand on the leader to help drag in the prize. Sharkers frequently facilitate this by using a "snapper line." This is a two thousand-pound-test nylon rope spliced to a heavy chrome swivel clip. The clip is snapped onto the leader-to-line swivel and the fishing line cut. Then everyone pulls on the rope. Sharks weighing several hundred pounds can be hauled up the sides of piers or bridges in this manner. An additional rope noosed around the shark's tail is also helpful. Another trick sharkers use for lassoing a shark when it is caught and wallowing thirty feet below them on a bowstring-taut line is to encircle the angler and rod with a large, sliding loop of stiff rope. The loop is dropped down the line and worked behind the shark's wide pectoral fins before it is tightened, and the catch hauled up.

Sharks brought alongside a boat at sea should not be brought aboard—for obvious reasons. They can be quieted by starting the boat's motor and dragging them backward on a tail rope until they drown. A close-range blast in the head with a shotgun is another way of dispatching them. Clubbing with a baseball bat is probably the least positive method of all. Clubbed sharks have been known to wake up later and wreck havoc, usually about the time the angler has his hands in its mouth trying to disengage the hook. If in doubt whether a shark is dead or alive, tap its eye. Any movement means life.

No matter where a shark is caught or how it is finished off, any angler who values all his limbs never forgets that a shark is a fully armed engine of destruction. These primitive fish die slowly, and until then are capable of inflicting considerable damage. But done properly, with these points in mind, shark fishing is no more hazardous than any other kind of fishing.

Taking the measurements of a dead shark is easy enough, but how do you weigh a catch that might tip the scales at several hundred pounds if you have no scales?

The International Game Fish Association has devised a mathematical formula for just such purposes. It will give you the weight in pounds of a shark or any other deep-bodied fish of similar shape. The formula is:

$$\frac{\text{Girth}^2 \times \text{Length}}{800} = \text{Weight}$$

Once shark fishermen fight their quarry into the surf, they often finish them off with a rifle shot to facilitate landing.

All this means is that the girth, or measurement in inches around the fish is squared (multiplied by itself). This figure is then multiplied by the fish's length in inches, and the result is divided by 800. The answer will be the weight of the catch in pounds. For example: If a shark's girth measurement, or circumference at its thickest part, is 64 inches, and its length from tip of snout to fork of tail is 90 inches, then, applying the formula:

$$\frac{64 \times 64 \times 90}{800} \text{ (or) } \frac{368640}{800} = 460.8 \text{ pounds}$$

Shark jaws make excellent trophies. The hardest part is cutting them out. Shark hide will dull the sharpest knife blade in seconds. And since shark jaws are not bone but cartilage, it is sometimes difficult to tell when you are cutting cartilage instead of meat. But once the jaws are removed, all surplus meat can then be pared away. Razor-sharp knives and a pair of pliers are used to cut away the gum coverings on the inside of both upper and lower jaws to expose the rows of concealed spare teeth. When all flesh is removed, the jaws should be soaked overnight in a solution made by dissolving half a pound of borax in a two gallon pail of water. This will remove all odor. The jaws are then spread wide and held open with two sticks wedged from top to bottom and from corner to corner. Two weeks of drying outdoors where they are protected from rain will harden the cartilage. After this the sticks can be removed and the jaws sprayed with clear plastic if desired. These sell for $25 and up.

Retrieving hook and end tackle from a shark is no easy job. Supposedly "dead" sharks have revived and wrecked havoc.

Despite the fact that shark fishing is increasing in popularity with sportfishermen, it is having the exact opposite effect upon people who profit from the tourist trade, particularly in such states as Florida. Too often sharks are cruising the same waters as surfers, bathers and divers. And occasionally one of these creatures bumps, bites or scares someone who had not bargained for that kind of treatment when he planned his itinerary for a restful Florida vacation. In effect, every time a shark opens its big mouth it gives the area a bad press for months to come. And a shark attack at a popular tourist beach can severely curtail business for the remainder of the season. This monetary loss to the tourist industry is calculated not in the thousands but in the millions of dollars, so it is understandable that some people who derive their livelihoods from tourists would prefer believing that no shark problem exists. Or if they admit that it exists, many insist that it has been exaggerated and overpublicized. The less action taken, the less done to attract attention, hence the less anyone will suffer. It is far easier to assume the attitude of the ostrich with its head in the sand than face up to the problem and all its possible consequences.

Unfortunately, it is this attitude that confronts and complicates the life of the shark fisherman. Along Florida's touristy east coast

While waiting for a run on his 16/0 reel, sharker Don McClure scrapes a set of jaws from a 10-foot Tiger shark he caught. Preparation of the trophies takes about two weeks.

certain piers and beaches are off limits to shark fishing. One pier owner near Jacksonville allows it only at night, providing the sharkers get rid of any disparaging evidence such as shark corpses before morning when the droves of tourist fishermen arrive. By day shark fishing is not allowed from this pier and other anglers are strongly advised against catching one either by accident or intent.

The Palm Beach Sharkers, an active club whose members were eliminating a large number of dangerous sharks from that resort coast, were put out of business by tourist interests. And for the last eight years the resort community of Fort Lauderdale by the Sea has had an ordinance that reads: "WHEREAS, fishing for, exhibition of, or landing of sharks, barracuda, or sting ray on the beaches of the Town of Fort Lauderdale by the Sea or the ocean waterways abutting said beaches is deterrent to the enjoyment of said beaches by the tourists, visitors and residents alike, and conveys the impression that said beaches are shark infested . . . it shall be unlawful for any person or persons to fish for shark, barracuda or sting ray, or exhibit shark, barracuda or sting ray or land shark, barracuda or sting ray on the beaches of the Town of Fort Lauderdale by the Sea. . . ."

Several years ago the ire of Florida's commercial mackerel fishermen against depredations of the shark came to the attention of fisheries experts at the Florida Board of Conservation Marine Laboratory at St. Petersburg. The problem was this: when gill-netters

(97)

laid their nets in the shallows half a mile offshore, expecting a rich harvest of Spanish mackerel, schools of sharks were ripping them open and stealing thousands of pounds of mackerel as well as ruining a lot of expensive nets. When the fisheries people studied the situation they came up with only one solution to the problem: increased fishing for sharks.

Four years ago, while addressing the annual convention of the Underwater Society of America, Dr. Donald De Sylva, of Miami's Institute of Marine Science, warned that the growing shark threat in southern Florida should no longer be ignored. It did go ignored, however, until April 20, 1968, when ten-year-old Steven Samples was attacked by at least three sharks while he floated on a plastic air mattress in five and a half feet of water twenty-five feet off Palm Beach Shores. The boy almost lost an arm and a leg and was bitten savagely on the back and buttocks. The surgeon who sewed Samples up said he took "literally hundreds and hundreds of sutures" to close the wounds. Since the boy was the third person to be attacked in a half-mile stretch of beach in six months, some of the local people were aroused.

Two weeks after the Samples attack, Congressman Paul Rogers invited four of the country's top shark authorities to meet at Palm Beach to discuss the shark problem. The panel included Dr. Donald de Sylva, Steward Springer of the U. S. Bureau of Commercial Fisheries, Captain H. David Baldridge of the U. S. Navy and Dr. Perry W. Gilbert, chairman of the Shark Research Panel. These experts recommended—to a man—that the Florida east coast communities should encourage shark fishing—especially commercial shark fishing—to reduce the shark hazard. Biologist Steward Springer said that by fishing for sharks the sports group called the Palm Beach Sharkers had been giving the area about $100,000 worth of free protection a year.

Despite the suggestions of these knowledgeable authorities, few community leaders did anything. Some, in fact, seemed anxious to make sure that nothing was done. But those who heeded the advice of the experts got busy and fished. In two nights of fishing half a dozen anglers hauled fifty sharks out of the surf off Riviera Beach, just north of where Steven Samples was attacked and nearly killed.

The next morning Riviera Beach was posted NO FISHING.

8

The Shark Specialists

The sea was calm, the day was hot and the wiry little man stalking down the beach with a big rod under one arm and a little boat under the other looked for all the world like a demented angler who had given up fishing for towing toy boats through the surf on the end of his fishing line.

But looks are deceiving. The angler was Herb Goodman of Lake Worth, Florida, a remarkably dedicated shark fisherman. Herb was no stranger to Boynton Beach that Sunday afternoon in mid-July. And the boat under his arm was no plaything. It was an ingenious device he built for launching baits, specifically shark baits in the two- to five-pound category.

The craft was thirty-six inches overall. Outriggers contained two six-volt Ray-O-Vac batteries for powering two small motors originally designed for bailing out a boat. Propulsion was by aluminum paddle wheels, one on each side of the hull. Inside the miniature vessel was an electronic guidance system that could be activated by a compact wireless transmitter from shore.

Herb propped his fiberglass Harnell rod and 12/0 Penn reel on shore, scooping a hole in the sand for the rod butt and bracing the reel with a slab of driftwood. He put the reel on clicker and paid out his 130-pound-test dacron line to the water's edge. At the end of the line was fifteen feet of flexible cable terminating in two 12-0 Sobey hooks, both firmly skewered into the bow and stern of a whole bonito weighing about seven pounds. If the belly of the bonito seemed to have an unnatural bulge it was because Herb had inserted half a sash weight, which would later hold the bait down. When everything was ready, Herb waded the boat and bonito just out beyond the riffling surf, loaded the bait aboard and set the craft adrift.

On shore he flipped the switch of the small transmitter and the boat's paddle wheels began churning. Slowly it moved out into deeper water, throwing up a small wake and towing the heavy leader and line behind it. The 12/0 chattered evenly and the dacron moved out through the guides.

Minutes later Herb squinted toward the tiny vessel that was now barely a white speck some three hundred yards from shore.

"That should do it," he said, and threw the reel in gear.

Line stopped. The bait dragged off the stern into the water. Herb manipulated the transmitter again and the craft executed a right turn and headed back toward the beach.

"Can't use the boat all the time," Herb told me as he snapped his reel out of gear and dropped down on the sand beside it. "When there's waves it doesn't work right. Can't keep it on course. Takes calm days like this, then she goes perfect." He peered out at the little boat homing in on us. "Now all we got to do is wait and see what happens," he said, smiling.

Things have been happening to Herb Goodman at Boynton Beach Inlet every Sunday for longer than he cares to remember. They all concern sharks, and the only thing that occasionally breaks up the routine is a giant ray. His most recent conquest was a nose-to-tail-tip fourteen-foot specimen that put up a two-hour battle and weighed about a thousand pounds.

Herb says he was born in 1898 in Detroit, Michigan, but the things the admittedly pint-sized angler goes through on a Sunday afternoon shark-fishing spree makes you realize that the man acts far younger than his seventy-plus years. He always wears a battered straw hat with a clutch of feathered jigs hooked to the front of the crown. His faded but still red sport shirt has the silhouette of a hammerhead shark stitched across the front, and in multicolored embroidered letters it bears the name of the small tackle shop he owns and operates in nearby Lake Worth. Without these trademarks it might be difficult to distinguish Herb from any other anglers plying the concrete jetties flanking the millrace waters of narrow Boynton Beach Inlet. But the shirt and the hat, plus the big fishing rig in the hands of the

At Florida's Boynton Beach Inlet, shark fisherman Herb Goodman displays a 10-foot hammerhead shark that he caught on bait launched by the small radio-controlled boat in the foreground.

sprightly little fellow with the quixotic grin, are always tip-offs that the one-man shark eradicator is at it again.

How successful he has been with his sport is a matter of record. It all started shortly after 1947 when Herb moved to Florida and got himself hooked on deep-sea fishing. One day he was out and had been fighting hard to boat a big one.

"It took me an hour and a half to get that fish in," he recalled, "and just as I did a shark took half of it." In angry frustration Herb hurled what was left of his mangled prize at the departing scavenger, and shouted, "You might as well take the rest of it!"

Later, in conversations with other fishermen, he frequently heard the remark that "little guys" seldom had a chance out there. If they couldn't boat their fish in a hurry, sharks usually took their catch away from them. Herb heard the remark once too often, then he decided to do something about it. He'd skip the other fish and just go after the sharks.

From that day on it has never gone easy for the 135-pounder. In the beginning it was catch as catch can and sometimes there was a question of who was catching whom. On one occasion, Herb, who has never mastered the art of swimming, hooked something so big that it pulled him into the surf up to his neck. Stubbornly refusing to let go of his valuable fishing gear, he hollered for help. Two skin-divers in a twelve-foot boat came to his aid and before he knew what was happening he was loaded aboard and heading out to sea towed by his fish. Four and a half hours later, several miles from shore, he still wasn't able to raise his ponderous catch off the bottom. The skin-divers were running low on fuel and so was Herb. He finally had to cut his line and admit defeat.

On more than one occasion the lightweight angler has beached a big shark only to have the creature smack him with its tail and knock him into the surf. And once, while accommodating a photographer, he straddled a supposedly dead ten-foot hammerhead. The shark revived, bucked him off its back and Herb still carried the bruises two weeks later.

Despite fifteen years of waging a lone vendetta against sharks, Herb never bothered to keep count of his conquests until ten years ago. Since then he has dispatched 160 sharks over six feet long. He doesn't count those under six. In fact he tries to avoid them by putting into practice the philosophy that the bigger the bait used the bigger the shark caught. All but two of these have been caught from the beach. His largest single catch to date is a twelve-foot-long 600-pound hammerhead. His largest multiple catch at one time is thirty—a female hammerhead that carried twenty-nine lively offspring. Still, many sharks that have Yo-Yoed Herb up and down the beach mercilessly have ended up escaping. And this becomes costly in terms of end tackle and line. But it has happened so many times to Herb that if he reels in a bare hook it often dredges up several hundred yards of line he lost weeks before. Since all this dacron comes in looking like the world's biggest tangle of spaghetti, it takes him weeks to get it unsnarled and on spools again. Sometimes when it is a particularly big mess he lays it out in his tackle shop and lets his customers have a go at it.

If medals were given for shark-fishing inventiveness, Herb Goodman would own a sizable collection by now. There is every indication that he may have been the first to use balloons for launching shark baits. Whether or not this is true, he has made some remarkable improvements on the method. Boynton Beach Inlet fronts on the Atlantic Ocean. The inlet is a narrow channel between two concrete jetties. A small bridge crosses the inlet where it enters the Intercoastal Waterway. The incoming and outgoing tides in this bottleneck are wild enough to make even the largest fishing cruisers crab back and forth to get through. When Herb can't use his radio-

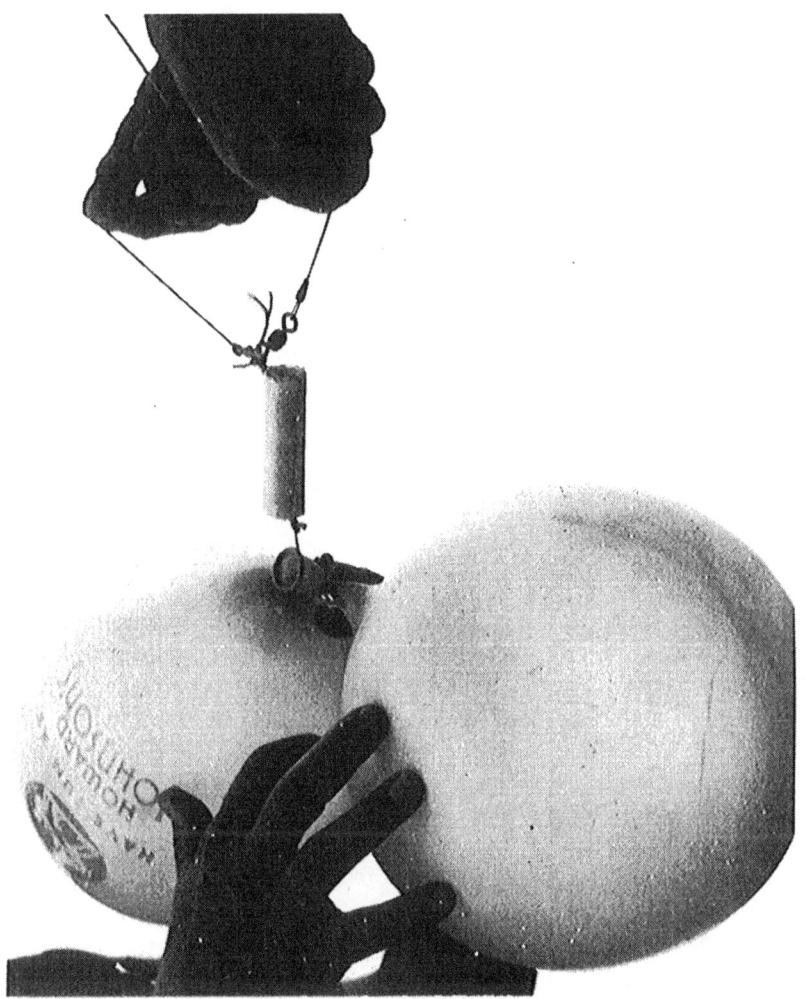

To launch heavy shark baits on an out-going tide, Goodman uses what he calls the "weak link." Balloons are joined to the angler's leader by a roll of Life Savers. They float the bait out to sea until the candy melts, letting the bait drop to the bottom.

controlled boat for launching, he uses the millrace waters of the inlet.

His baits are usually a pair of three-pound bonitos or jack crevalles with sash weights in their stomachs. Two twelve-inch balloons are tied with a quick release knot to his leader swivel. The whole rig is then carried by a friend out to the end of the south jetty while Herb pays out line and carries his rod out to the end of the north jetty. While the friend holds onto the end tackle, Herb strips several hundred yards of his line into the outrushing waters where it bellies into a huge bow. Then at a given signal Herb's companion releases the ballooned baits from the south jetty. The currents literally snap them through the inlet like the knot on the end of a whip. When they are out where he wants them, Herb jerks his rod. The balloons pull free and the sash weights carry the baits to the bottom, where they will rest until a passing shark comes along.

Jerking the balloons loose from the end of four hundred yards of limber fishing line is not as easy as it sounds. When Herb tired of it he put his mind to work and came up with what he calls a "weak link" launch. To his leader swivel he attaches a line that is run through a roll of Life Savers and back to his swivel again. A second line is looped through the Life Savers and on this two balloons are tied, the loops linked only by the candy. When this combination goes seaward the bait is buoyed by the balloons until the candy melts; dropping the rig to the bottom. Herb figures he gets a ten-minute float out of a roll of Life Savers, longer if he leaves on the paper wrapper.

Herb's bait had been soaking for almost two hours when the 12/o's clicker suddenly uttered a high-pitched stutter, the kind that automatically snaps your heart up where your Adam's apple belongs.

Herb bounced off the beach and scooped up the rod in one movement. The butt went between his legs, his left hand gripped a handle clamped ahead of the reel to keep it from wobbling (Herb disdains fighting harnesses) and he crouched waiting while the 12/o sang. He waited while the shark ran, waited to give it plenty of time to gulp the bait well back into its gullet. Then he threw the reel in gear and struck.

The Harnell arced, the drag jumped two octaves and Herb bent backward with his heels digging sand.

In the next hour and a half there were times when the big reel looked as if it were stripped cleaner than an apple core. That's when Herb sweated most and redoubled his effort to gain line. But after each heave, crank and pant routine that inevitably fattened the spool, the shark in turn seized every opportunity to reverse the process. And during these exchanges Herb alternately crabbed backward up the beach or was dragged reluctantly back to the water's edge. At least once he was up to his armpits in the surf.

When the shark lay heavy on his line, Herb urged it into action to keep it moving, to keep it tiring. When gradually he began gaining line that the shark did not steal he had to winch it in by degrees, winning it with the kind of effort guaranteed to leave his back muscles with the painful memory a week later.

The dark swatch in the water came closer, then the up-thrust, widely spaced dorsal and caudal fins broke the surface.

"It's a hammerhead!" Herb wheezed excitedly. "Big one at that!" He was as jubilant as a boy with his first catch. He led the boat-length shadow into shallow water, then handed me the rod.

"Keep a taut line while I handle the gaff, get me?"

I nodded as my sweaty hands gripped the Harnell and put a steady strain on the dead weight in the surf. Herb advanced with his gaff, an eight-foot staff as thick as a baseball bat with a meat hook adorning one end and a heavy manila rope wrapped around its shaft. In knee-deep water he sank the hook on his first swipe. The shark set up a rumpus that felt like it was trying to jerk my arms out of their sockets. But through the froth and foam came Herb, hauling triumphantly on the end of the rope with every ounce of energy he could muster. Then the crowd of bystanders that had swarmed to watch the fight lent him a hand and with their help Herb's hammerhead shark —all ten and a half feet of it—came sliding up the sand incline clicking its teeth and pounding the beach every inch of the way.

Herb studied his catch thoughtfully, wiped his glasses, happily posed for photographers, then glanced over at me with a grin.

"While this one's cooling off, what say we go get us another?"

That invitation said more for the man and his sport than anything else. Herb Goodman is a shore-based shark-fishing specialist. He has solved some of the most difficult problems of the sport by sheer ingenuity. If you were to ask him why he goes to so much trouble, he would be the first to admit that it isn't all done solely for the purpose of eliminating sharks. The fact is he likes it. He likes the challenge, the excitement, the rough-and-tumble fight and the crowd it attracts—the people who can't quite believe what they see this spunky little man in a natty straw hat haul out of the ocean on a Sunday afternoon. He doesn't have a fancy boat, nor do his catches have the revered reputations of sailfish or marlin. But no one who has ever seen him in action will ever doubt that Herb Goodman's sport isn't big-game fishing in all its glory.

Almost two hundred miles to the north of Boynton Beach is

The end of a menace—on the point of a shark fisher-man's gaff hook.

Sebastian Inlet and some of the sharkiest waters I've ever fished. When a news item reported that many large sharks had been seen patrolling the mouth of the inlet, that was all the encouragement a fellow sharker and I needed to go there. Sebastian Inlet proved to be another rampaging channel similar to Boynton Beach Inlet. On canoe-launched baits fished from the beach we caught three tiger sharks up to ten and a half feet long, two bulls and an eight-foot lemon shark in an afternoon. That night we lost several others and had both our reels stripped of eighty-pound-test line by sharks too large to handle from shore. Apparently the outrushing waters of the inlet were producing plenty of food for the number of sharks gathered at its mouth. This fact, plus the carcasses of our half-day catch, prompted an old-timer to question the wisdom of a man he said he had seen paddling out the inlet that morning on what he supposed was a surfboard. When I asked a local tackle dealer about this I learned that the "surfer" was Ben Logan, a local kayak enthusiast. The reason the old-timer had not noticed the little fabric-covered boat was because the inlet was too rough.

Ben Logan is a heavily tanned, muscular two hundred-pounder whose idea of fun is to stalk and catch tarpon and sharks from the dubious safety of his cockleshell kayak. Like all kayaks, Logan's

Florida Shark Club member, Bob Fudge, opens the cavernous mouth of a 10-foot 6-inch tiger shark he caught at Florida's Sebastian Inlet.

boat is unsinkable, has a low center of gravity and is double-ended. Propulsion is by muscle power and a double-bladed paddle. He has equipped the single-seated cockpit with a rod holder so that he can troll lures about one hundred feet astern, using a heavy rod and about five hundred yards of sixty-pound dacron line on his 6/0 reel. With this combination Logan has caught some extremely large fish. But sometimes it seems that it is the fish that is doing the catching.

During a typical fishing trip, Logan, a civilian technician at Cape Kennedy, may roam thirty or more miles offshore, frequently in tow to a huge shark that could easily shred his fifty-eight-pound boat and its occupant as well. But Logan bears sharks no malice. He catches them strictly for sport and goes along for the ride. When the sharks weary of the fun it's Logan's turn to tow. He paddles them ashore, and if they are not mortally injured he releases them. One catch towed him through a storm. When he came out under clear skies he was eight miles at sea. Another time, Logan realized too late, that his catch was a giant manta ray.

"Next thing I knew I was launched straight up, boat and all," he recalled. His rod was jerked out of his hand, then he came down —hard. "All I could think of was sharks and that I had tied the paddle to the boat. Otherwise I'd have been up the creek."

Logan's fishing trips may keep him at sea anywhere from an hour up to several days. One night during a fifty-mile paddle along the coast to New Smyrna, he got hungry and opened a can of tuna. As he held it over the side to drain off the oil he spotted an enormous convoying shark in the moonlight, its jaws about six inches from his hand.

"I didn't argue," said Logan wryly. "I just dropped the can."

In over twenty years of deep-sea kayak fishing along Florida's east coast Logan has caught and bested hundreds of sharks from his cockleshell craft. However, it is a method not recommended for the average angler. So far Ben Logan has been successful, but along with that success he knows the true meaning of knock-down, drag-out battles with big sharks.

Another specialist who believes in giving sharks a sporting chance is Scotty Slaughter, a blond, blue-eyed skindiver from Clearwater, Florida. One dazzling summer day Slaughter slipped into the turquoise blue waters off Key West, Florida, for an enjoyable afternoon of shark hunting. With him he carried a five-foot metal pole and a meat grinder. A couple of fathoms below the surface he calmly stuffed chunks of a freshly killed seven-foot sting ray into the meat grinder and cranked out a cloud of minced bait that slowly drifted downcurrent. Soon he had five hungry sharks gliding around him. One, a seven-foot dusky shark, seemed more excited over the prospective meal than did the others. It broke away from its companions and began swimming tighter circles around Slaughter. Suddenly, maddened by the tantalizing scent of ground ray, the shark flicked its powerful tail and bore down on Slaughter, jaws agap. The skindiver raised his metal pole like a jousting lance and rammed it against the onrushing shark's head. There was a water-muffled concussion, a blast of bubbles and the shark's lifeless body sank with a fist-sized hole where its brain used to be.

Scottie Slaughter's deadly weapon was a "powerhead"—a steel tube on the end of his metal pole armed with a twelve-gauge shotgun shell. When he rammed the shark with it the shell jammed back against a pin in the powerhead that detonated the charge. Contact concussion and a massed load of number 8 birdshot did the rest.

Slaughter's technique for dispatching sharks is both simple and lethal. Operating to depths of one hundred feet without special breathing apparatus, he has used his powerhead to kill more than one hundred sharks, including hammerheads and great whites.

As often as he has come close to making a meal for a shark, none was closer than the time he stalked a seventeen-foot great white shark that was swimming just below him. Slaughter angled down to make his kill. Just as he lunged with his powerhead, the white swung its head. Instead of hitting a vital spot, the charge merely stunned the killer. Lacking a second shell, Slaughter flippered for his boat at top speed. Reloading, he turned just as the man-eater charged, "with his mouth open like a cellar door." Slaughter slammed his powerhead into the gaping maw and ended the encounter not a second too soon.

Of all men who have earned the respect of their peers by pitting their skills against the greatest fighting fish nature can provide, few have set their sights so high and made their mark so well as Alfred Dean of Australia. When Dean isn't tending his small vineyard he is usually on his boat in the Great Australian Bight, a wide bay of the Indian Ocean, trying to catch the largest game fish in the world. How successful he has been is a matter of record. Dean has caught the four largest fish ever taken on rod and reel, breaking his own world record each time. All of the fish were great white sharks and each weighed more than a ton. But like so many fishermen, his really big catch was the one that got away.

Australians call Alfred Dean's biggest shark Barnacle Lil. She is a female great white but she is no lady. She has broken the hearts of many an Australian fisherman since the moonlight night that Dean met her while fishing on the Great Australian Bight. What had attracted her was the tantalizing scent of whale oil and steer's blood that dripped from a tank in the stern of Dean's boat. The mixture formed a chumming slick on the water that sharks could home in on from miles away. Barnacle Lil made her presence known by banging the bottom of the boat, then tearing off a seal carcass, something Dean often hangs over the stern as an added inducement. As she munched her meal on the surface a short distance away, Dean avidly eyed her measurements. He estimated that she was over twenty feet long and weighed at least four thousand pounds.

Quickly he baited two large hooks with seal liver, then lowered another seal carcass over the stern near the hooks. In one furious lunge Barnacle Lil swooped in and gulped everything—the seal, the hooks and part of the boat's transom.

Dean climbed into his fighting chair—a tractor seat bolted to the deck—and went to work. The shark streaked out several hundred yards of line on her first run, then turned and rocketed to the surface, lifting her huge white shape almost clear of the water before thundering down, smashing the sea to lather with her giant caudal fin. Then she concentrated all the controlled fury of her four thousand pounds in a savage fight against the man and his rod. It was a fight that lasted two hours before Dean's straining arms and aching muscles finally worked the shark in foot by foot until she was close enough to the boat for the mate to grasp one end of the fifteen-foot wire leader.

But Barnacle Lil was far from finished. With a sudden violent burst of speed she broke away and took with her all the line Dean had painfully gained. The fight continued. Three times he forced Barnacle Lil to the side of the boat and three times she found renewed strength to get away. Two more hours elapsed and Dean's hands slowly turned to a pulp. His fingers felt as if they had been pulled loose from tendons and joints. Blisters swelled and burst until little more than raw flesh clutched the bobbing, straining rod. As the fight went into its fifth hour Dean's back and legs twitched with painful muscular spasms; he began suffering acute stomach cramps. Finally, after five and a half hours, he fought Barnacle Lil to boatside once again.

The mate reached for the leader and drew it in. Five . . . then ten feet of the glistening wire were aboard. Then Barnacle Lil made her last bid for freedom—she sounded. As she dove straight down, the leader caught on the boat's pipe railing and whisked it over the side, tearing out a seven-foot chunk before the wire snapped.

Alfred Dean, the man who holds the all-tackle, rod and reel world record for catching the largest fish—a sixteen-foot ten-inch great white shark weighing 2,664 pounds—lost his greatest catch. Since then other anglers have sighted and pursued her, but no one has ever caught Barnacle Lil. She still swims free on moonlight nights in the Great Australian Bight.

9

Schoolmistress of Sharks

One afternoon in November 1958 a small, darkly attractive young woman carrying a pail of fish in one hand and a notebook and stopwatch in the other walked out a dock overlooking a fenced-in lagoon near Placida, Florida. In the calm, slightly murky water before her two sinister shadows undulated up from the bottom and circled warily around the enclosure. They were nine-foot lemon sharks, a male and a female. In the deeper water, seeming almost reluctant to move out of the gloom, were three male nurse sharks, each about nine feet long.

The young woman, dressed in a sport shirt and Bermuda shorts, was Dr. Eugenie Clark, director of the Cape Haze Marine Laboratory and one of the most knowledgeable authorities on sharks. She had trained the five sharks in the lagoon to play a game involving eating. All they had to do was push a target that rang a dinner bell— and food would be served immediately to them. What interested Dr. Clark was exactly how and why her sharks played the game. Did they associate the bell-ringing with the food-getting? Was memory involved? Were the sharks able to communicate among themselves during the game? What would happen if she changed the rules? These were the things Dr. Clark hoped to learn. With this knowledge scientists could forge one more link in their understanding of shark behavior. And that link might lead to a positive method of shark control.

Normally, few women would choose to specialize in a field where all her subjects were ruthless, cold-blooded killers, especially if she knew she was expected to capture these killers before her real work even began. But not Dr. Eugenie Clark. She chose sharks because to her they were remarkable creatures of which little was known. There was a need for research, a need for knowledge about them. That was the challenge. As for the hazards, she was one woman who was not exactly a stranger to danger, be it in the form of poisonous fish or marauding sharks.

Eugenie Clark's interest in these things began at an early age. She was born in New York. Before she was two years old she made frequent trips to the beach with her mother, who was a swimming teacher. When she was nine Eugenie had her first introduction to fish in the old New York Aquarium, where she spent each Saturday while her mother worked. This led to a tropical aquarium of her own, and she eagerly became a young collector of fishes, snakes, toads and lizards—the whole menagerie kept in an assortment of cages, boxes and jars in the Clark's small apartment.

Later Eugenie went to Hunter College and majored in zoology. Her research work in ichthyology for her master's degree led to a research assistant's job at the Scripps Institute of Oceanography at La Jolla, California, where she became an avid skindiver. And while working on her Ph.D. at New York University she spent several years researching the reproductive and behavioral habits of tropical fish at the American Museum of Natural History. Eugenie's specialized knowledge in this field made her a logical choice when the Office of Naval Research selected her for a one-woman mission to the Pacific to study poisonous fishes. In the Palau Islands, southeast of the Philippines, she perfected her skindiving and spearfishing techniques under the tutelage of an expert native diver named Siakong. It was on dives with Siakong that she learned to cope with the many hazards of the undersea world—the dangerous sharks, the vicious moray eels, the man-eating clams. Siakong later disappeared during a dive and was never seen again.

After eighteen months in the Pacific, Eugenie returned to New York to receive her Ph.D. as an ichthyologist. A Fulbright Scholarship took her away again for a year to study fish in the Red Sea. When she returned this time it was to write a successful book about her underwater adventures in far-off seas. The book, *Lady with a Spear*, attracted the attention of Alfred and William Vanderbilt, who were interested is establishing a marine laboratory on Florida's Gulf

Dr. Eugenie Clark (left) and an assistant measure
the pectoral fin of a Great White shark at the Cape
Haze Marine Laboratory.

Coast. They offered Eugenie the directorship of the laboratory and
she happily accepted. When the Cape Haze Marine Laboratory
opened in 1955, Eugenie took charge and got busy learning everything she could about sharks.

In the beginning her main problem was how to catch enough
healthy subjects for her research. Sharks in their natural environment
are tough, healthy, practically indestructible animals whose only natural enemy is man. Capturing them and transferring them from the
sea to shark pens at the laboratory without harming them proved to
be a more delicate operation than one would suppose. The sharks were
caught easily enough on a five-hundred-foot shark line anchored at
both ends and containing fourteen hooks on dropper chains along the
middle three hundred feet. In six years Eugenie caught more than
three hundred sharks this way, but each morning when she checked
the line few of the sharks would still be alive. Towing the live ones
back to the laboratory from almost three miles at sea often drowned
them. Nor could they easily be lifted aboard the research boat. Once

sharks are hoisted out of water by their tails their bodies lose much of their support and their internal organs are crushed by their own weight.

Assistants on Dr. Clark's shark-collecting team finally devised a "live car"—actually a boat-shaped floating live well with a removable stern gate and slatted bottom for water circulation. Catches were pulled into the live car without removing them from the water. After that sharks could be brought back to the laboratory in one third the time it took before, and they were in far better shape.

Once safely inside a holding pen at the laboratory, the newly captured specimen often looked more dead than alive. It would sink to the bottom and refuse to swim. Handlers would then get into the shallow end of the pool and "walk" it around the enclosure to circulate water through its gills and revive it. Once the shark came out of its stupor, the handlers lost no time getting out of the water.

Dr. Clark learned quickly that sharks are not the gluttonous eaters we often suspect them of being. One nine-foot tiger shark did not begin eating until five days after it had been caught. A ten-foot tiger shark at Marine Studios did not start until it had been in captivity for five months. But Dr. Clark found that once large sharks began eating, three feedings (fifteen pounds of fish) a week were sufficient to keep them in good health. When water temperatures dropped from the 70s to the 60s, the sharks often stopped feeding for days, weeks and even months before resuming.

In the earlier stages of shark collecting she and her assistants often captured small nurse sharks by skindiving, grabbing these sluggish sharks by their tails and dragging them ashore. Most catches were under three feet long. When an assistant attempted the same thing with a five-foot specimen, it turned and bit him on the leg. In captivity almost all sharks developed aggressive tendencies, even the usually docile nurse sharks. One of the shark maintenance men, stooping over the feeding platform in the shark pen, had the tip of his finger nipped off by a supposedly harmless nurse shark.

The five sharks Dr. Clark selected for her behavior experiments were well adapted to captivity. They were healthy, active, alert specimens that fed well and were responsive. During a six-week training period these sharks were fed five times a day and always at the same time. At each feeding a white plywood target sixteen-inches square was lowered into the water with the sharks. The target was built in such a way that whenever it was pressed back more than two inches it rang an electric bell underwater.

Day after day food (about five ounces of mullet or jack) was gradually thrown closer to the target. Finally it was attached to the center of the target on a weak string. To get the food into its mouth the shark had to press the target and ring the bell. At the end of the six-week training period Dr. Clark was ready to find out if the sharks had learned to associate the target with the food.

At the beginning of the seventh week an empty target was lowered into the water at the regular feeding time. When a shark pressed the target with sufficient force to ring the bell it was rewarded with a piece of fish dropped into the water to one side of the target. Ten seconds were allowed for the shark to get the food. If it was not taken by that time the food was removed. Each week the food was dropped a little farther from the target. The sharks' responses and reaction times were closely noted and recorded. In less than a week both lemon sharks had learned to press the target in order to get the food.

Dr. Clark's resulting data brought out some interesting features in the sharks' behavior. During the early phases of the training, for example, she found that the sharks were capable of hovering before the target. This was indicated by their ability to steal food seventy-five times from the target without moving it the two inches required to ring the bell. She also noted that, although both the lemon sharks rang the bell and obtained food at the target a total of 522 times, there was a strong tendency for the male to approach first while the female held back until the male satisfied its hunger. Over an eleven-week period the male lemon shark rang the bell first fifty times out of fifty-three feedings, even though the female was often closer to the target than the male.

To see how well the sharks remembered what they had been trained to do, Dr. Clark stopped the experiments in mid-December when the water temperatures in the pen dropped and the sharks ceased feeding. In mid-February temperatures were up to normal and the target was again lowered into the water. The sharks rang the bell in the usual manner. This indicated that Dr. Clark had succeeded in developing in them a conditioned reflex (a learned response) or behavioral pattern that required a certain action (the pushing of the target and the ringing of the bell) before the shark could proceed to reap its reward (the food). This was further substantiated by the frequency with which the sharks often bypassed food in order to ring the bell *before* they allowed themselves to turn back and take it.

If such conditioning of sharks is possible, then there is room to speculate on its practical application. Could all sharks somehow be psychologically conditioned or trained to avoid humans? Dr. Eugenie Clark's dinner-bell experiments indicate that possibly they could if a way were found to do it. An interesting postscript to this research occurred on the day she changed the rules of her bell-ringing-for-food game. To test the sharks' ability to perceive color and to note their behavioral adjustability, she substituted a yellow target for the usual white one. The shark charged, then swerved violently aside without striking it. Instead, it flipped backward out of the water and rushed to the other end of the enclosure where it behaved neurotically. The shark refused food presented to it in any manner and died of starvation a few months later. That slight change was enough of a shock to result in its eventual death. "This incident and other experiments that followed lead one to suspect that sharks are more delicately balanced than was thought," said Dr. Clark. "Perhaps also that an effective way to repel sharks is to upset one of their routines."

Behavioral experiments were only part of the various research programs that Dr. Clark carried out at the Cape Haze Marine Laboratory. In eleven years she dissected and studied over two thousand sharks. Repeatedly she acted as midwife to shark mothers, delivering as many as thirty-seven shark pups by cesarian section from a single shark. This was an effort to keep newborn sharks alive in captivity to learn when they reached maturity—an elementary fact, perhaps, but one we knew nothing about. Unlike bony fish, sharks do not have scales that show annual growth rings. However, scientists are presently studying what they believe might be growth rings in shark's vertebras. At least one shark in an Australian aquarium is known to have lived twenty-five years in captivity.

When Dr. John H. Heller, director of the New England Institute for Medical Research, found that an organic chemical distilled from shark liver oil might combat heart disease, he went to Cape Haze. Dr. Clark assisted in this research, helping Dr. Heller inject live captive sharks with the chemical—squalene—that had been marked with radioactivity so that its progress could be traced through

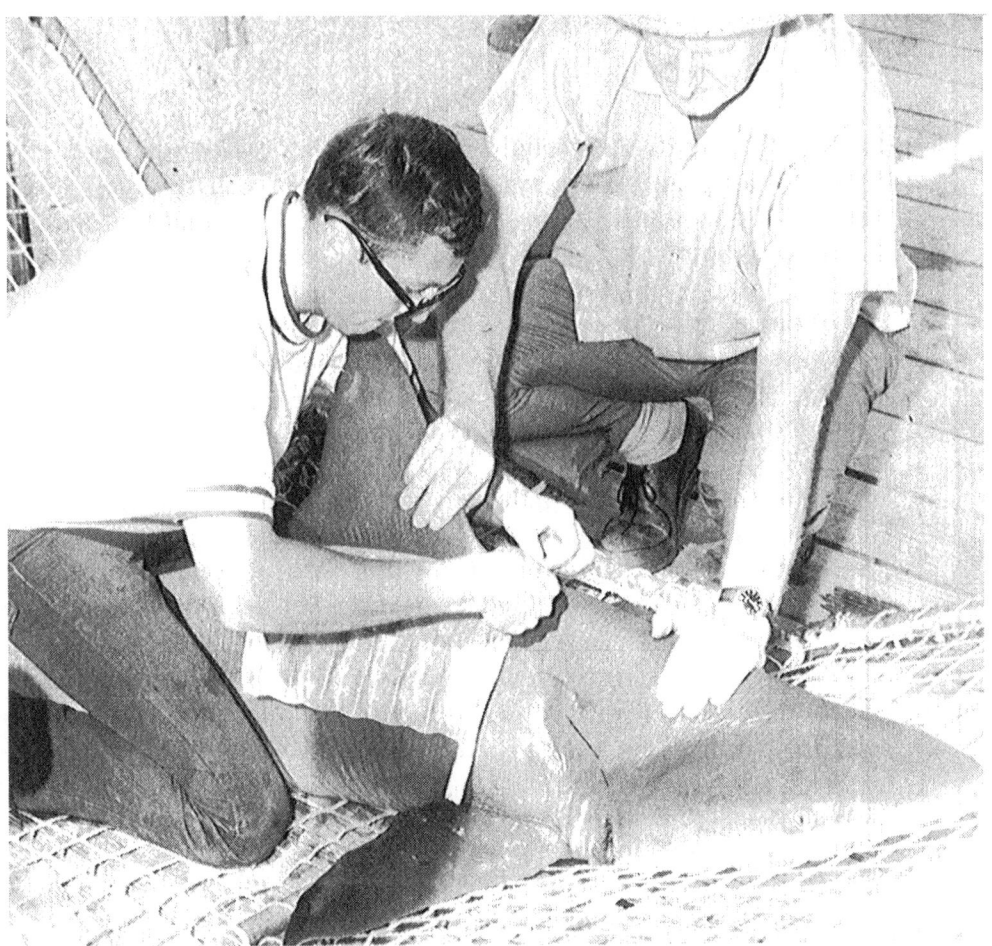

Dr. Perry Gilbert watches as an assistant attaches a saddle to the back of an anesthetized brown shark. The less sharks eat the more they weigh in the water, therefore, by adding lead weights to the saddle, scientists are in effect artificially starving the shark to learn how it responds.

the shark's body. The experiments failed, but scientists have not given up on squalene. More recently it has been tried on experimental animals with remarkable results, increasing the body's resistance to infectious and parasitic diseases as well as malignant tumors. Some believe that squalene might be the key to a cancer cure.

For a lady who knows so much about sharks, Dr. Clark is often asked that one vital question: "What should I do if a shark swims near me?"

"Whenever someone asks me that," she said, "I tell them it might be best to swim toward the shark to send it away. Most of them are really cowards. Another thing to remember is that just because you spot a fin cutting the water, it doesn't mean a shark is going to attack. Sharks usually swim completely under the surface and you don't see the fin. Most large fins reported seen in warm seas turn out to be pectoral wing tips of harmless manta rays. Your chances of running into an aggressive shark are infinitesimal. Millions of people swim in salt water every year, and there are billions of sharks in the sea, yet the number of authenticated attacks in American waters during the average year can be counted on the fingers of one hand."

For skindivers she has this advice: "In my opinion, a skindiver completely submerged in clear water is in relatively little danger. Even if a shark is hungry—and they go for days without feeding—the fish generally takes its time investigating a possible meal before sampling it. A diver wearing a face plate can see as well or better than the shark and almost always has time to get out of the water. And I do recommend that you get out when faced with an aggressive shark—particularly if you have speared a fish and there is blood in the water. A diver has absolutely no defense against a large shark which means business. Don't panic—move slowly. A swimmer can't outrun a shark, so don't do anything to excite it."

The Cape Haze Marine Laboratory is now supported largely by the Mote Scientific Foundation and grants from the National Science Foundation and the Office of Naval Research. It is presently called the Mote Marine Laboratory under the executive directorship of Dr. Perry W. Gilbert. Dr. Eugenie Clark alternates between teaching at the University of Maryland's Department of Zoology, in College Park, and continuing her shark studies at the Mote Marine Laboratory as time permits.

10

Porpoises vs. Sharks

At least twice a month Dr. Gilbert receives a letter from some interested party who thinks that he or she is making a constructive suggestion in saying "Since the porpoise is known to be the sworn enemy of the shark, why don't you and the AIBS Shark Research Panel study porpoises to find out what there is about them that frightens sharks away?"

The porpoise is not a fish but a warm-blooded, air-breathing mammal of remarkably high intelligence. There are twenty species roaming the waters of the world and they are all related to the whale. Wherever porpoises are found, these playboys with their built-in smiles have earned impeccable reputations of being among the friendliest of creatures to man. Even the ancients recognized this quality in them. They called the porpoise a dolphin, which until present times has caused the mammals to be confused with the true dolphins, which are fish. But no matter what his name, they knew him as friendly. Plutarch, the Greek biographer (A.D. 46–120), wrote, "He is the only creature who loves man for his own sake. Some land animals avoid man altogether, and the tame ones such as dogs and horses are tame because he feeds them. To the dolphin alone, nature has given what the best philosophers seek: friendship for no advantage."

Everything we know about porpoises is remarkable. They swim incredibly fast, can herd fish, kill sharks and communicate with each other. They possess the keenest hearing, the sharpest sense of humor and the most sensitive sonar equipment of any animal in the sea. They are highly intelligent and their brains are so similar to the human being's that some scientists believe they may be taught to talk.

Porpoise families are very close. They are highly protective of their young and often it is at these times that they have trouble with sharks. For a shark sometimes makes the mistake of attacking a baby porpoise. When this happens the youngster emits a piercing cry for help. Instantly the adults rush to the rescue. Since porpoises lack powerful jaws, their only weapons are their speed, weight and the battering-ram bluntness of their hard heads. Without hesitation they hurl themselves headfirst into the offending shark, ramming him in the gills and body. The encounter is short, swift and deadly. With ruptured internal organs, the shark soon spirals toward the bottom to die. Regrouping, the porpoises speed on their way with their youngster merrily riding the bow wave close to his mother's head.

In his book *Shark! Unpredictable Killer of the Sea*, Thomas Helm describes a memorable encounter between a pack of porpoises and a large hammerhead shark.

Helm and his companion had just launched a dinghy from a sloop and were about to go scallop hunting near Caladesi Island in the Gulf of Mexico when they noticed a disturbance in the mirror-slick water between them and the beach.

"Scrambling to the cabin top, we saw nearly a dozen shapes darting about in the clear green water. As we watched, a big hammerhead, which must have measured better than fourteen feet in length, shot up into the air. He had been hit from below by a big porpoise.

"Hardly had the hammerhead crashed back into the water when a second porpoise bore in and sent him rolling like a birled log. Time after time the shark was struck by the porpoises. Once the besieged prey and one of his attackers met almost head-on and they both erupted from the surface.

"Bob and I realized that we were witnessing a real battle royal between a herd of bottle-nosed porpoises and a big hammerhead shark. Why the battle had begun could only be guessed.

"Before the next few minutes passed, we counted ten porpoises swimming in a circle around the fourteen-foot hammerhead like a band of Indians around a covered wagon. Every few seconds one of the porpoises would break out of the circle and rush the shark. Now and then the hammerhead's jaws must have made contact with one of the attackers, for there was the unmistakable sign of blood in the clear green water.

"Suddenly the big hammerhead leaped almost clear of the water again, and when he splashed back in he seemed to relax; then he drifted aimlessly toward the clear sandy bottom. The porpoises continued to circle, with first one and then another diving down to give the lifeless carcass an exploratory bump, and then, as if following some order, they turned seaward."

In November 1965 at Washington, D.C., fifteen of the top scientists and shark authorities in the United States held a conference to discuss the shark-porpoise relationship. What the public did not know was that certain scientific work had already been done on this subject. The purpose of the conference was to review these findings and to determine what more might be done.

Is it true that porpoises and sharks are deadly enemies? Are they really the "cats and dogs" of the sea as is so widely believed?

Panel member F. G. Wood, who at that time was with the Marineland Research Laboratory at St. Augustine, Florida, said, "The answer to this question does not seem to be a simple one. There's no reason to doubt accounts of fishermen who have reported seeing vicious battles between sharks and porpoises, but there is evidence that the two do not invariably tangle when they meet.

"Some of the things we need to know, and don't, are what kinds of sharks are involved in these battles? What causes a fight to start? Who initiates the hostilities? Obviously, it is difficult to obtain answers to these questions by making observations in the open sea. The chances of being at the right time and place when a fight begins must be very small."

Wood added that the large circular oceanarium at Marine Studios was a good facility for observing the reactions of sharks and porpoises when they were put together. In the files of the Marineland Laboratory were notes left by the first curator, who described two incidences when sharks were put into the tank with the porpoises. On each occasion the porpoises quickly attacked and killed the shark by butting it in the body and gill region with their tough, hard snouts.

"Some years ago we thought we'd see for ourselves what happens when a shark is placed in a tank with porpoises," said Wood. "We tried several different kinds of sharks, including tigers. Each time the result was the same. After showing considerable excitement, the porpoises settled down and generally ignored the shark, though some of the younger and more playful animals amused themselves by swimming rapidly across the shark's bow or nibbling at its tail. None of the sharks seemed to pay any attention to the porpoises, aside, perhaps, from speeding up to escape a tormentor. . . .

"We've long assumed that a shark attack is very unlikely if a school of porpoises were playing close by a human being in the water. But, not long ago, a friend of ours reported seeing a large white-tipped shark, one of the most dangerous kinds, swim through the midst of a school of porpoises with no apparent notice on the part of the fish or the mammals.

"It appears that we still have a great deal to learn about the relationship between sharks and porpoises."

Fishery biologist Stewart Springer, of the Bureau of Commercial Fisheries, described a situation he had observed in which porpoises were victims of sharks.

"We were loafing along at three or four knots," said Mr. Springer, "washing down the deck after a frustrating early morning purse seine set that caught little except jellyfish, when about fifty porpoises came and maneuvered close against the ship's side. This was unusual because we were moving too slowly to give them any sport. They were the usual kind of mid-Gulf of Mexico, *Delphinus*, and their behavior was startling. It was obvious that these porpoises were dead tired and some were injured. By looking closely we began to see the dim shapes of sharks staying perhaps thirty yards away from our boat and the porpoises. There were six or eight quite young porpoises, not more than three feet long, and these were herded in close to the boat while some of the large ones patrolled the fringe of the porpoise school that now had our vessel to protect one flank.

"The porpoises trusted us with their young and our 250-ton tub of a fishing vessel responded as well as it could. We tried stopping, but this seemed to bring the sharks in and to disturb the porpoises, so we went ahead as slowly as possible, slower than big diesel engines like to go. Someone thawed some frozen fish and tried to feed the porpoises, but they appeared to be too exhausted to be interested. Now and then a shark would burst into a series of dashes. We could not see whether any contact was made between the porpoise and sharks. The sharks always retreated but did not go away. Some of the patrol porpoises had been injured. Several were scarred and one had a badly shredded tail fin.

"There was no real evidence that the sharks were cooperating. They were working independently—each one making separate attacks. Given a little intelligence or some pattern of cooperative attack, there seems little doubt that the sharks could have finished the action in short order, and, at least, could have eaten the young porpoises as well as any last-ditch defenders.

"It was easy to see that the porpoises were cooperating and that they were not only protecting their young, but also were protecting each other. One shark would not have given the porpoises much trouble, but a large group of sharks had seriously endangered the entire school of porpoises and possibly had already decimated it.

"We felt badly because we could not do anything about the sharks and we didn't feel like abandoning the porpoises. Our dilemma was resolved in about an hour by a small but violent rain squall. When we came out of it the porpoises and sharks were gone. Perhaps the short rest and the surface disturbance caused by the squall allowed the porpoises to escape with their young."

To study the relationship of sharks and porpoises under controlled conditions at the Lerner Marine Laboratory in Bimini, Robert F. Mathewson and Dr. Gilbert ran a series of experiments in the laboratory's shark pens.

The test animals were one tiger, three lemon and three dusky sharks; the porpoises were two adult, recently captured and untrained females. During the tests twelve hundred feet of color motion pictures were made of the action while a record of the sonic signals emitted by the porpoises was obtained with a tape recorder and hydrophone.

In the first test one adult lemon shark was introduced into the observation pen containing one adult porpoise. The two animals were of similar size. As soon as the porpoise observed the intruder, it emitted startled, "chirp-like" noises. The porpoise appeared to be genuinely alarmed. It raced about the pen and, after a few minutes, advanced toward the lemon shark and emitted "clicking" sounds. The lemon shark, which had momentarily deviated from its course around the side of the pen, returned to its former course. At no time did the porpoise make contact with the shark, but it appeared effectively to

Like most sharks, the broad wing-like pectoral fins of this tiger shark helps it maneuver and support itself in the water. Unlike most sharks, this species can rest momentarily on the bottom, ventilating its gills without moving.

cause it to change course by swimming directly toward it, usually approaching from the side, and emitting a series of "clicks."

When another lemon shark was let into the pen with the first, the porpoise was no longer as excited as it was in the beginning. During subsequent tests in which various numbers and species of sharks were let in with both porpoises, the results were always the same. The porpoises occupied the entire central part of the pen and effectively kept the sharks along the sides with "clicking" sounds whenever the sharks strayed toward them.

From these tests Mathewson and Gilbert found these points noteworthy: (1) A new alarm signal was recorded from a single porpoise when the first lemon shark was introduced into the pen. (2) Porpoises appeared to utilize sonic signals in locating a shark moving toward it. (3) Once the porpoises closed in on a shark, the sonic signals often ceased. It appeared that the presence of the porpoise at close range was sufficient to cause the shark to change course. (4) At no time did a shark make an aggressive pass at, or contact, a porpoise.

This visual and tape-recorded evidence was presented at the conference on the shark-porpoise relationship. In summing up that discussion, these were the main points made: (1) There is much fictional but little factual data on shark-porpoise behavior. (2) Neither shark nor porpoise is a major food, nor a common prey, of the other. (3) Observations at sea and in controlled laboratory experiments substantiate stories that porpoises can drive sharks away. (4) If porpoises are to be utilized in work in the open sea, such as SEALAB, it is desirable to know how porpoises react to sharks and whether it may be necessary to allow for interference by sharks that would jeopardize what a porpoise is trained to do. (5) More acceptable than a research proposal that states, in effect, "We are going to train a porpoise to kill a shark," would be a thorough study of the way in which various environmental factors, including sharks, influence the behavior of porpoises. Such a study, properly planned and executed, would tell us a great deal about animal behavior and intelligence in general. (6) It may be desirable to study the reaction of different species of porpoises to sharks. There may also be one species of porpoise that is more aggressive and more trainable than others. This then becomes a screening process—a very time-consuming undertaking. (7) Any research program undertaken along lines suggested in points 5 and 6 above should be funded for at least three years. It is estimated that the cost of such a program will be about $40,000 per year.

11

Science and Sharks

Almost everything we know about sharks has been learned since 1942. At that time the government launched a wartime crash program to find a suitable shark repellent. The result was Shark Chaser —a nigrosine dye, copper acetate compound. After the war subsequent tests found it disturbingly unreliable. While some sharks were repelled by it, others were unaffected. As the shark menace grew, so did our concern. In 1958 the American Institute of Biological Sciences and the Office of Naval Research called a conference of world-wide shark authorities and scientists at New Orleans' Tulane University to discuss the problem. In two days of discussions it was generally agreed that we knew too little about "the enemy." We needed a better understanding of the biology and behavior of sharks before satisfactory countermeasures could be taken. To implement this need the AIBS Shark Research Panel was formed. Under the direction of Dr. Leonard P. Schultz, a Shark Attack File for the world was carefully compiled and studied for patterns of similarity that might reveal why attacks occurred. To date this list contains nearly fifteen hundred documented case histories on file at the Mote Marine Laboratory in Sarasota, Florida. Captain H. David Baldridge is presently coding this information for computer analysis.

Research programs designed to fathom the mysteries of sharks were begun on an international scale. As a direct result of these efforts we have learned more in the last eleven years about sharks than has been learned in the last two and a half centuries.

At Florida's Cape Haze Marine Laboratory, Dr. Eugenie Clark

expanded her shark-conditioning experiments to include studies of how well sharks could differentiate between various shapes and colors. She presented a lemon shark with a diamond and a square target, rewarding it with food when it pressed its snout against one and punishing it by bumping its snout when it pressed the other. Although both targets were white, the shark had little difficulty learning the difference between the two. It did have difficulty, however, when presented with a circular and a square target, both white. Apparently it could not distinguish between these shapes. However, the same shark learned quite easily to distinguish between a red target and a white target of the same shape. Did the shark really see the colors? Dr. Clark believed that it responded to brightness.

In retrospect, these facts come to mind: pioneer commercial shark fisherman Captain William E. Young found that he could attract sharks to an area by dropping sheets of white newspaper on the surface of the sea. Wartime survivors reported shark attacks on life rafts painted yellow. More recently, when Dr. Albert L. Tester and Dr. Perry W. Gilbert were testing the plastic survival bag called Shark Screen, sharks were attracted to light-colored bags having high reflectivity, but turned away from dark-colored bags. And it might be well to remember what La Jolla, California, skindiver Robert L. Pamparin was wearing when he was devoured by a great white shark in 1959: blue swim fins, black face mask; pink swimming trunks, white gloves and he carried a yellow-handled abalone iron. Whether sharks see colors as we do, or merely respond to their brightness, scientists believe they are a contributing factor in shark attacks.

At the Lerner Marine Laboratory on Bimini Island in the Bahamas, Dr. Gilbert ran exhaustive tests on various chemical and mechanical repellents. One such device was the bubble curtain, once believed to be an effective barrier against sharks. A perforated rubber hose was layed on the ocean floor around the beach it was to protect. Compressed air pumped through the hose created a curtain of bubbles that was said to frighten sharks so badly that they refused to pass through it. In 1960 some New Jersey resort owners who had protected their beaches in this manner were certain that the bubble curtain was the answer to the shark threat. Dr. Gilbert was not so sure. In two large shark pens at the Lerner Laboratory he tested the device on twelve adult tiger sharks from five and a half feet to thirteen feet long and weighing ninety-five to nine hundred pounds. Eleven of the sharks swam back and forth through the bubble curtain as if it were not there. The twelfth tiger shark was repeatedly repelled by it. Had Dr. Gilbert worked only with that one shark, his findings on the effectiveness of the bubble barrier would have been different. This incident pointed up the need for many tests on many kinds of sharks under all manner of conditions.

When Dr. Gilbert tested the copper acetate, nigrosine dye compound called Shark Chaser, the sharks avoided the bluish-black cloud of dye that stained the water of the pen. Was it the odor of the copper acetate that repelled them? Or were the sharks frightened by the dark cloud of dye they could see? When the dye alone was used the sharks continued to avoid it, retreating to the far side of the pen until literally cornered there by the expanding dark cloud. Could they perhaps smell the dye? Dr. Gilbert anesthetized a test shark and plugged its nostrils. The shark still avoided the dye. But when the shark was outfitted with opaque plastic eye shields, which prevented it from seeing, it swam straight through the dyed water.

Further experiments at Bimini demonstrated the importance of vision in the feeding behavior of sharks. A shark that could see had no difficulty locating a bait. When the shark was fitted with eye shields it had great difficulty locating its food. Beyond a ten-foot range of food in turbid water, however, it was proved that the shark relied on its sense of smell or hearing.

Ralph E. Sheldon, working at the Marine Biological Laboratory in Woods Hole, Massachusetts, was the first to demonstrate scientifically that smell plays an important role in guiding sharks to a meal. He found that sharks had no difficulty distinguishing between a cheesecloth packet of crushed crab meat and several identical packets of pebbles. But when he plugged their nostrils they failed to home in on the food packet even when they swam close to it. When one nostril was unplugged the sharks had no difficulty adapting to the situation and eventually they found the food from among the decoy packets.

How acute is the shark's sense of smell? Scientists have evidence that, with a strong current helping disperse a scent, sharks can detect the odor a mile from its source. It is only a question of how much scent is diluted in the water. Lemon sharks were able to detect the odor of tuna juice seventy-five feet from its source when the juice was diluted one part to 1.5 million parts of water.

In 1962 at the University of Hawaii, SRP member Dr. Albert L. Tester reported that several species of sharks showed a mild response when water was siphoned into their tank from another in which fish were swimming. When these fish were agitated, the sharks in turn developed an agitated attraction to the siphoned water. This suggests that frightened fish may give off some substance in sufficient qualities to attract sharks to them. Tester's findings raised another question for future research: When humans are frightened or in distress do they exude a similar scent substance that may incite sharks to attack?

Why do sharks attack humans in the first place? Is it from hunger, as we have long believed? Or is there another motivating force? Naval biochemist Captain H. David Baldridge, attached to the Mote Marine Laboratory, recently offered this new theory: A significant fraction of shark attacks on man may well be the result of an aggressive rather than a feeding behavior. Baldridge noticed that in numerous cases of shark attack there was evidence to indicate that some sharks had used their razor-sharp teeth as weapons in a way totally unrelated to the procurement of food.

The early 1968 attack on young Steven Samples near Palm Beach, Florida, was one such example. Samples was attacked by at least three sharks and almost lost his life. Yet each of his swim fins showed clear, crescent-shaped impressions of contact with shark teeth, *but on one side (the bottom) of each fin only.* It would have been impossible for the fins to have been placed in a position so that a single bite could have produced the sets of impressions on both fins at the same time. Furthermore, severe wounds on his legs appeared to be cuts or slashes without matching puncture wounds of the shark's other jaw, as would be expected in a true bite. Singular wounds of this type have appeared on other victims as well as on sharks in captivity. This tends to indicate that not all sharks bite to devour, but perhaps rush in with open mouths to rake their victims, using their teeth in anger rather than to procure food. Baldridge feels that such attacks might be brought about when victims accidentally interfere with the courtship patterns of sharks or bring out their aggressive tendencies in other ways. If this is true, then our search for effective repellents, which has been based on discouraging the hunger drive in sharks, must be re-evaluated.

If sight and smell lead sharks to their prey for either a fighting or feeding attack, how important is their sense of hearing? Are there certain sounds that attract sharks?

These were the questions confronting Dr. Warren J. Wisby of the University of Miami's Institute of Marine Science when he began research on the relationship of sharks and sound in 1961. Nearly sixty years ago Dr. George H. Parker of Harvard University found that a shark deprived of its sense of sight·and hearing would still continue to respond to a source of disturbance in the water as long as its lateralis system—the line of sensory pores along its sides— remained intact. When Parker severed the main nerve trunks of this system, however, the shark ceased to respond. Just how sensitive this complex listening device is and at what distances the shark can detect various disturbances under water was unknown until Dr. Wisby and his associates conducted a series of unusual experiments that began to shed light on the mystery.

Dr. Wisby remembered that many skindivers and fishermen reported that they never saw sharks around until after they speared or caught a fish. Then the sharks would arrive. And oddly, they often came from up-current, a direction from which they could not have smelled the fish or its blood. This suggested that sharks were not only attracted by a certain quality of sound, but that they could locate its source in three-dimensional space. But how?

Wisby decided that the first step was to find out what kinds of sound were made by struggling fish. With the help of graduate students Donald R. Nelson and Samuel H. Gruber the experimenters went out to the reefs off Miami armed with a tape recorder and a hydrophone (an instrument for detecting sounds underwater). Using scuba gear, they located a large black grouper in a cave. While one of the divers placed the hydrophone near the cave, the other speared the fish. The sound of its struggles was tape-recorded by an operator in the boat.

Back at the laboratory the sound was analyzed and found to be composed primarily of low-frequency sound waves. These were then reproduced and recorded in three forms: as low-frequency pulsed or interrupted sound, as high-frequency pulsed sound and as low-frequency continuous sound.

The next step was to return to the reef and play. back the recording through a transducer (a special kind of underwater loudspeaker) to see how it affected sharks.

Results were amazing. The boat anchored near the reef in forty-five feet of water. The transducer was lowered over the side on a long cable and an observer in the water positioned himself on the surface above it. The tape recorder was switched on and the sounds played for periods of fifteen minutes with variations of intensity every ten to fifteen seconds. When the low-frequency pulsed sound was played sharks appeared where none were before and swam directly toward the transducer, approaching it as close as three feet. When they found no food they veered off and either left the area or circled at a distance. During a nine-day period, eighteen sharks up to nine feet in length, including hammerhead, bull, lemon and tiger sharks, were attracted to the low-frequency pulsed sound—essentially the same sound made by a struggling fish or a thrashing swimmer. Not only did the sharks easily home in on the sound but they were able quickly to locate its source from as far away as six hundred feet. The low-frequency continuous sound did not attract sharks. And only two were attracted to the high-frequency pulsed sound, which the scientists believed may have been due to some low-frequency noise that was also on the tape.

The results of these experiments bore important implications. They proved that sharks in their natural environment could be attracted by certain sounds. Since the main attraction was to low-frequency pulsed sound it appeared that not all sounds that sharks could hear would attract them. In the laboratory it was found that a shark's hearing range was from 7.5 to 400 cycles per second (cps). Dr. Wisby believed that they used only the lower part of this range, from 7.5 to 100 cps for hunting, which meant that sharks were able to hear many sounds that humans could not. Human hearing ranges between 40 cps and 2,000 cps. Struggling fish or humans transmit bursts of low-frequency sounds whenever they thrash about. These bursts of sound travel through water at a mile a second and they apparently act as a "dinner bell" on any shark within hearing.

Today the work started by Dr. Wisby is being carried on at the University of Miami Institute of Marine Science by Dr. Arthur A. Myrberg and others. They are trying to learn more about how sharks hear and how they use this faculty to find their prey. Sound travels through water about five times faster than it does through air. Even though sharks have ears, they are spaced too closely together to allow for any kind of "hearing triangulation"—the ability to pinpoint the location of a sound by hearing it from two widely separated positions. And, unlike other fish, a shark lacks an air bladder, the internal organ that not only helps him float without swimming at any desired depth, but is also believed to serve the fish as a kind of resonator for amplifying sounds. How then do sharks manage this trick when they seem so poorly equipped for it?

In seeking the answer scientists recalled the early work of Dr. George Parker, who had found that sharks deprived of their sense of smell and hearing could still respond to disturbances, providing their lateralis systems were left intact. It has long been known that these sensory cells along the shark's sides were sensitive to low-frequency sound waves, but no one understood the significance. Now scientists believe sharks use this unique sensory system to home in on sounds by "feeling and interpreting" pressure displacements set up by the low-frequency sound waves. All sound travels through flexible mediums such as air and water in a series of high and low pressure waves. High pressure means that the molecules or water particles are compressed, or squeezed together. Low pressure means just the opposite; the particles have been displaced, or moved away. A displacement measuring device revealed that sharks sense this movement rather than the pressure itself in determining the source of a sound. Only future research will tell us how sensitive this homing device is and exactly how the shark uses it. In the past we believed that splashing water near a shark would frighten it off. Now we no longer do. What these new findings mean is that any unnecessary splashing or thrashing about in the water could invite a shark attack, and therefore should be avoided at all costs.

In the last few years a wide range of new research has been in progress. Through the assistance of private and governmental grants, investigators are now probing deeper into the mysterious functions of sharks than man has ever gone before. Currently there are more than 150 different shark research programs in progress at fifty different universities and research institutions throughout the United States. At Cornell, Miami and Hawaii universities, scientists are doing advanced work on the specialized sensory systems of sharks.

At Miami, research assistant Samuel Gruber designed an ingenious device for studying a shark's vision. An experimental shark is secured to a platform in a tank of circulating water. One end of the tank is a plexiglass bubble into which the shark's nose is fitted.

Outside this window a researcher flashes a small, filtered light of various colors and intensity. Each time the light flashes a mild electric shock causes the shark to blink. This is repeated until the shark becomes so conditioned that it blinks whenever the light is flashed, indicating that it can see the color and intensity of light being used. With this approach Gruber and his colleagues have learned that color perception in some sharks is highly likely. The knowledge of which colors they can see best and which colors they can see poorest would be invaluable to swimmers, victims of sea disasters, and manufacturers of garments and gear for use in the sea.

In laboratories at Cornell, Plymouth and the Scripps Institute of Oceanography at La Jolla, California, Dr. Gilbert and others have minutely studied the structural makeup of the shark's sight and smell organs. One outgrowth of this research has been the discovery of a unique structure in sharks' eyes that provide them with the unusual ability to tell the difference between an object and its background in extremely dim light.

Elsewhere scientists were interested in learning exactly how hard a shark could bite. At the Lerner Laboratory in Bimini, and at the Mote Marine Laboratory in Florida, Dr. Gilbert found out by using an instrument with a name that is a mouthful in itself. It is called a gnathodynamometer, or "bite-meter," a remarkable device designed by James Snodgrass of the Scripps Institution for measuring the power of a shark's jaws.

The bite-meter is a cylinder containing an aluminum core of known hardness. This core is enclosed by four quadrants of steel supported by twelve stainless-steel ball bearings. Bait fish is wrapped around the bite-meter and it is offered to a large shark. The shark bites down hard on the apparent meal, then releases the unpalatable morsel. By knowing how much force is required to dent the aluminum core, Dr. Gilbert can tell how much pressure was behind the bite.

He has given the bite test 175 times to large lemon, dusky, nurse and tiger sharks. These tests have revealed that the biting pressure of an eight and a half-foot dusky shark is about *eighteen tons per square inch!*

In oceanographic instrument work, sharks have long been suspected of biting in two thick synthetic fiber and steel cables. It appears now that they are fully capable of such damage.

It is well known that a shark's jaws are filled with hundreds of

razor-sharp teeth and that replacements are readily available whenever the creature loses a tooth. But how often does a shark lose a
tooth? Dr. Gilbert's recent research on the structure and function
of shark jaws turned up the amazing fact that the average life of
a shark's tooth in the outer row of the upper jaw is only 7.8 days.
In the outer row of the lower jaw it lasts only 8.2 days. This is a
much more rapid rate of tooth loss and replacement than anyone
had hitherto believed.

In California scientists are gravely concerned over the dangers
of shark attack to some 114,700 certified scuba- and skindivers in
that state. Each year 14,000 new divers, including both militarily
and commercially trained aquanauts, enter the watery world of the
shark and expose themselves to these dangers. To learn how great
the potential shark threat is Gilbert W. Bane, at the University of
California, is conducting a shark census of the area. His primary
concern is with such known trouble-makers as the great blue shark,
the hammerhead, bonito and great white shark. Commercial longline
fishing methods are being used to learn the distribution and den-
sities of the shark population. Related studies concern the migratory
habits of sharks, the concentration and location of food fishes that
may attract them, the changes in weather, water and current conditions—all factors known to have some bearing on the incidence of
shark attacks.

In this relentless search for more knowledge about sharks nothing
is being overlooked as a possible clue to their strange behaviors, not
even their parasites, the tiny animal organisms that may live on or
in them. Roger Creasey of the Smithsonian Institution and Professor
Murry D. Dailey of the California State College at Long Beach
are involved in a world-wide investigation of the geographic distribution of parasites found on sharks. By learning more about the
parasites, scientists hope to learn more about their hosts, the sharks.
For example, a shark is occasionally caught in shallow inshore waters
harboring a parasite normally found on oceangoing sharks. This indicates a possible shark migration from open-ocean to coastal areas.

At the Mote Marine Laboratory at Sarasota, Florida, Dr. Dudley
Klopfer of Washington State University is testing the higher learning
abilities of sharks. It is called discrimination reversal learning because
once a test shark is trained to do one task (press a target for food),
it is then required to do another (press a second target for food).

At the Mote Marine Laboratory at Sarasota, Florida, a shark pen and shark moat hold live sharks used in scientific research. Pens are separated by an observation stand.

As soon as it learns to do the second task, it is rewarded only when it again does the first task. How quickly the animal learns to tell the difference between the two tasks it must perform to be rewarded will determine how quickly the shark can adapt to changing situations. This and similar tests will in turn tell investigators more about the shark's intelligence.

In Southern California biologist Donald R. Nelson and electronic engineer Howard Carter plan to attach ultrasonic-transmitting devices to sharks so that their locations and activities can be followed at sea with directional radio-receiving equipment. Sensors will be built into the transmitters to relay water temperature, depth and swimming speed of the sharks. Using this technique, investigators hope to learn more about the behavior of sharks in their natural environment.

In 1958 when Billy Weaver, a teen-age surfboard rider, was fatally attacked by a shark off Lanikai, Oahu, in the Hawaiian Islands, community leaders and government officials decided to see if intensified fishing methods would cut down on the shark hazard. A sampan was chartered and outfitted with Japanese longlines—mile-long lengths of nylon rope containing up to twenty-three hooks tethered at intervals along the main line. Three such units were to be anchored or buoyed around the island and fished periodically for a year by the sampan. Among the species caught on the vessel's first circuit of the island were thirty-three tiger sharks. Twenty-nine were brought in on the second trip, eleven on the third trip and nine at year's end, on the fourth and last trip. When the successful year-long experiment was over, 694 sharks and 641 pups had been destroyed—proof that continued fishing pressure would decimate the shark population.

As of June 1967 a similar shark-control and research program has begun as a cooperative effort between the University of Hawaii, the State Division of Fish and Game and the Oceanic Institute. Under the guidance of investigators Albert L. Tester, Kenji Ego and others, six months of longline fishing has already eliminated about 350 large sharks from seventeen adjoining inshore areas around the Island of Oahu and two outside areas off other nearby islands. Tester is fishing seventy-two hooks a night for one to three nights four times a year. The program is expected to last for three years and one of its primary goals is to measure the effect of fishing on the prevailing shark population.

Until recently we have known little about the populations, growth rates and migratory habits of sharks. But now shark-tagging programs in this country and abroad are slowly filling in the picture for us. No matter where it is done, tagging sharks is not an easy job. First the shark must be caught on rod and reel. This means that the tagger may be in for as much as a two-hour muscle-straining fight before his patient is quiet enough for the operation. And a freshly caught big shark at boatside is seldom very quiet. It is a wildly twisting, rolling, thrashing, jaw-snapping creature that knows no calm. While an assistant handles the fishing gear and tries to hold the catch alongside, the tagger prepares to tag. The dart tag is a yellow plastic streamer attached to a pointed, stainless-steel head. Printed on the streamer is an identification number and a request that when the shark is recaught the angler mail the tag back to the laboratory along with information on how, when and where it was caught. This tag is attached to the end of a six- to ten-foot pole that serves as a hand harpoon. The tagger aims for a target area at the base of the shark's first dorsal fin, then thrusts downward hard. A quick pull frees the harpoon. The tag remains in the shark's hide. The leader is cut and the shark released.

One of the most active shark-tagging programs in the United States is being carried on by research biologist John G. Casey of the

Department of the Interior's Bureau of Sport Fisheries and Wildlife. In 1961, Casey began tagging sharks between Maine and Chesapeake Bay. With the assistance of shark-fishing enthusiasts, the operation soon spread down the Atlantic coast. Results have been impressive. Casey and his team of sportsmen have tagged over six thousand sharks. Nearly two hundred have been recaptured. In 1966 the most remarkable recoveries were from juvenile sandbar sharks tagged on nursery grounds in Virginia in 1965. These sharks were recaptured in December off North Carolina, in March off Florida, in May again off North Carolina, and in June in the Virginia area where they had been tagged the previous year. These results supported the belief that this species migrated south in the winter and returned to northern nursery grounds each summer. But Casey's most dramatic recoveries came in 1968 with blue sharks that had made almost unbelievable long range migrations. One of these, tagged off Martha's Vineyard, Massachusetts, on July 15, 1968, was recovered four months later off Barbados in the West Indies, 2,700 miles away. The shark had traveled an average of 22.5 miles per day, *every day for four months!*

An equally interesting project relative to the migratory movements of sharks is in progress at Lake Nicaragua, Central America. For years it was believed that the fresh-water sharks of Lake Nicaragua were landlocked there by a series of rapids in the river linking the lake to the sea. Now there is evidence to indicate that some sharks may travel up the twisting, 130-mile-long, rapids-filled San Juan River to the lake. To prove this theory Professor Thomas B. Thorson of the University of Nebraska is tagging sharks at the mouth of the river and hopes to recover them in the lake. Besides using conventional tags, Thorson has attached sonic tags—miniaturized radio transmitters—to eleven sharks at the mouth of the river. These are being tracked from a boat with a hydrophone and receiver. Several stationary shore monitors will be placed at strategic points in the delta area to record passage of the sonic-tagged sharks if and when they make the up-river trip.

These are but a few of the current research projects designed to broaden our knowledge about sharks. Until now these animals have been thought of as our enemies—primitive and menacing barbarians from out of the past. But what of tomorrow? Recent scientific findings indicate that, despite their evil reputations, sharks may prove to be our benefactors of the future.

12

Barbarian or Benefactor?

Until now everything that has been discussed about sharks has had
to do with either their physical uniqueness or their barbaric natures
and man's attempts to combat or comprehend both. Despite all our
efforts, the shark threat is still a very real problem. And it appears
that there will be no simple solution, no absolute safeguard, no
magic pill to instantly shield us against attack. In the last eleven
years more than two hundred chemical compounds have been tested
for their deterrent effects upon sharks, and not one compound, including Shark Chaser, has proved totally effective. Recently, Captain
H. David Baldridge, USN, has conclusively demonstrated that no
drug, even of high toxicity, will provide satisfactory control for aggressive sharks in the open sea. So science is directing its attention
away from chemical deterrents and seeking answers elsewhere. One
of these new directions concerns making a beneficial use of sharks as
laboratory animals.

In the last decade sharks have been used more and more as
experimental animals for solving problems of the human body and
its organs, to study viruses and their control and for seeking new
methods and substances to protect humans against disease. Through
experiments on the spiny dogfish, scientists at the Mount Desert
Laboratory, Maine, have contributed significantly to our better understanding of the human kidney and the processes by which the body
converts food to its needs. A dozen investigators at the National
Institute of Health now regularly use sharks as the experimental

animals of choice in their various research programs. At the Lerner Marine Laboratory, Drs. L. William Clem and Michael Sigel, collaborating with Dr. Parker A. Small of the National Institutes of Health, discovered that sharks possess only one class of serum antibodies. These are similar to those a human infant produces to protect itself against disease, and those which adult humans produce in comparable quality only when afflicted with certain blood cancers. It could be of importance to learn how sharks make up such high levels of these proteins.

Through studies of shark brains, blood and livers, at the Mote Marine Laboratory, Drs. Richard H. Adamson and David P. Ralls of the National Cancer Institute are trying to learn: (1) how sharks absorb, distribute, use or eliminate various drugs introduced into their systems; (2) how effective is the cancer-inhibiting factor found in the plasma of sharks, particularly nurse sharks, on various forms of blood cancer; (3) how cerebrospinal fluids form and circulate in the shark, so that we may better understand the mechanics of this process in man.

The functional relationship of mother to developing young has been explored in a variety of viviparous sharks by Franklin Daiber and his graduate students at the University of Delaware and by Dr. Gilbert and his graduate students at Cornell University. Doctors and scientists from the U. S. Naval Medical Institute, UCLA Bone Research Laboratory, Variety Children's Research Foundation, Dow Chemical Corporation, Institute of Neurological Diseases and Blindness, National Institute of Mental Health and the National Heart Institute are but a few of those who are making significant contributions to our medical and scientific knowledge by using sharks as experimental animals. Through research programs such as these, sharks are making their most important contributions to man.

In many countries of the world sharks have long been recognized as an economical asset. In England and Australia the fish in "fish 'n' chips" may be school shark. In Europe, Africa, Mexico, Central America, South America and Asia, shark is considered an excellent food fish, which in fact it is. The nourishing, high-protein meat is sweeter and milder-flavored than some of the more commonly sought food fish. In Mexico shark meat is dried, salted and sold extensively. In Japan shark is used in no less than twenty-five different dishes, including the famous shark-fin soup. Recent statistics compiled by the Food and Agriculture Organization of the United Nations reveals that sharks comprise about 1 percent of the present world market for fish. Interestingly, the shark enjoys its greatest popularity not only in those countries where food is in short supply, but also in those that are noted for their fine cuisine.

In the United States, however, it is limited as a food fish, and few people knowingly eat shark. Many eat it unknowingly, for the meat of some sharks so closely resembles the delicious flavor of swordfish that it is frequently sold as its substitute. Many housewives have paid $1.60 a pound for a choice filet of swordfish at their local fish markets and received instead a choice filet of shark. There is little difference in quality. Mako shark is most often the swordfish substitute, with the snowy white, slightly dryer meat of the blue shark running a close second. Other people prefer young black-tip, nurse or lemon sharks when they know what they are eating, and smoked bull shark is so delicious it has to be tasted to be believed.

One day Americans may cultivate a taste for sharks. If this were to happen, increased commercial fishing for them would not only help cut down on the burgeoning shark population but the shark menace as well. As one writer so aptly put it, "If people were to demand shark instead of some other fish at every restaurant where they ate, who knows what could be accomplished? In so doing, the life they saved might be their own."

Years ago, when it was learned that the shark's ponderous liver was rich in vitamin A, commercial shark fishing in this country during the 1930s and '40s became a big industry. Although the vitamin content varied from one liver to another even among the same species of shark, in the heyday of the industry the oil content of a single large hammerhead's liver could net a fisherman $500. The need for vitamin A was so great that the Borden Milk Company operated a shark-fishing fleet of its own. And the soupfin shark, which not only possessed an unusually large liver but was also much sought after for its choice fins used in the making of shark-fin soup, was hunted almost to extinction. In its best ten years, a commercial shark fishery at Salerno, Florida, took more than 100,000 sharks from the waters of the Florida east coast. But during World War II, when we learned how to synthesize vitamin A cheaply, the demand for shark liver oil ceased and the industry folded. Since then the shark population has been on a steady increase, and so have the depredations it causes.

Today there is little commercial shark fishing done in this country, but for those few who still stick with it, the value of a single tiger shark around twelve feet long is about $30. In perfect condition the hide is worth a base price of $12.50, plus a 50 percent bonus because tiger hides are top quality; at 7¢ a pound, the meat will bring about $10.00; the relatively small fins of this shark, another $3.00. Although this may sound profitable, shark fishing is a risky profession where losses through hide damage or spoilage and just plain bad luck take a heavy toll on the profits.

Once the sharply pointed "skin-teeth," or denticles, are removed from a shark hide and it is tanned, it becomes a leather with a tensile strength several times that of cow or pig leather. It is scuff-proof and extremely durable. The Ocean City Leather Company of Newark, New Jersey, is the exclusive tanner of shark leather in this country. Its main products are shoes, belts and briefcases made of shark leather. Prior to 1964 the company processed sixteen thousand shark hides annually, its supply coming mainly from shark fisheries in Mexico, Cuba and other countries in the Caribbean. But since 1964, with a change of ownership, new sources of supply and more demand for top quality shark leather, Ocean Leather has processed sixty-five thousand hides a year and still is having difficulty meeting the demand for its products.

For centuries the shark has been a menace to man. It may continue to be. But daily we are learning more about this unique creature, learning to live with it and to cope with it. Once science and industry fully exploit its useful features, there is reason to believe that the shark will be less of a liability and more of an asset to man. And in the future the shark may prove to be a greater benefactor than man has ever dreamed.

APPENDIX I

The first step in making an identification is to establish that the animal is in fact a shark. A shark has—

- 5 to 7 paired gill openings located at least partly on the sides of the head;
- a skeleton composed wholly of cartilage;
- jaws, teeth and paired fins;
- a body shape that is typically fusiform, that is, torpedolike (the exception is the angel shark, which is flattened);
- a skin that, being covered with minute toothlike scales, has a sandpapery texture.

These features help distinguish sharks—

- from lampreys which lack paired fins and true jaws;
- from skates and rays, in which the body is flattened and the gill openings are entirely on the undersurface of the body;
- from bony fishes, which have only one pair of gill openings;
- from whales and porpoises, which lack gills and scales.

When you are sure that the fish is a shark, the next step is to see how it differs from other sharks in this region. Sharks are distinguished by shape, by size, and often by the presence or absence of certain anatomical features.

* From *The Angler's Guide to Sharks*, Circular 179, Bureau of Sport Fisheries and Wildlife.

(142)

A dependable method is to use the key. This is a series of alternative descriptions which lead, by successive choices, to the correct identification. It is always necessary to begin at the beginning, that is, with the first pair, 1A and 1B, and follow the directions through the key.

IDENTIFICATION KEY

The key is a series of *couplets*, or paired descriptive statements that give contrasting characteristics. In each couplet you are offered a choice between two descriptions; select the one that best fits the shark you are examining. That selection will either name the shark or refer you to another couplet. As successive choices are made, the characteristics become more specific. For example, in identifying the smooth hammerhead your path through the key would be 1B to 2B to 5A to 6B to 7A. The important point to remember is always begin at the beginning and follow every step until you find the proper name.

1

A. Body flattened; pectoral fins broad and winglike
=Atlantic Angel Shark
B. Body rounded, torpedo-shaped. *Go to couplet 2.*

2

A. Anal fin absent. *Go to couplet 3.*
B. Anal fin present. *Go to couplet 5.*

3

A. Spine in front of each dorsal fin. *Go to couplet 4.*
B. No spine in front of either dorsal fin =Greenland Shark

4

A. Origin of second dorsal fin behind the pelvic fins
=Spiny Dogfish
B. Origin of second dorsal fin over the pelvic fins
=Portuguese Shark

5

A. Head expanded sideways like shovel or hammer. *Go to couplet 6.*
B. Head not expanded sideways like shovel or hammer. *Go to couplet 9.*

6

A. Head shovel-shaped   =BONNETHEAD
B. Head hammer-shaped. *Go to couplet 7.*

7

A. Front margin of head not notched at midline
                          =SMOOTH HAMMERHEAD
B. Front margin of head notched at midline. *Go to couplet 8.*

8

A. Free rear tip of second dorsal fin shorter than the vertical
    height of fin   =GREAT HAMMERHEAD
B. Free rear tip of second dorsal fin longer than vertical height
    of fin   =SCALLOPED HAMMERHEAD

9

A. Tail about as long as entire length of body. *Go to couplet 10.*
B. Tail much less than length of body. *Go to couplet 11.*

10

A. Rear tip of first dorsal fin terminates in front of pelvic fins
                          =THRESHER SHARK
B. Rear tip of first dorsal fin extends at least as far as the pelvic fins
                          =BIGEYE THRESHER

11

A: Keel or ridge on sides of caudal peduncle. *Go to couplet 12.*
B. No keel or ridge on sides of caudal peduncle. *Go to couplet 17.*

12

A. Keel a weakly developed ridge; caudal peduncle nearly round; lower lobe of tail less than half as long as upper lobe. Go to couplet 13.
B. Keel strongly developed; caudal peduncle flattened; lower lobe of tail ⅔ as long as upper lobe. Go to couplet 14.

13

A. Origin of first dorsal fin about opposite rear margin of pectorals; body gray, often with irregular dark bands or spots
=TIGER SHARK
B. Origin of first dorsal fin well behind pectorals; body blue, no dark bands or spots
=BLUE SHARK

14

A. Gill slits long—extend almost full height of head and nearly meet on under side of head
=BASKING SHARK
B. Gill slits shorter—do not extend full height of head or very far on under side of head. Go to couplet 15.

15

A. Second keel below and to rear of main keel; teeth with two small auxiliary points at their base
=PORBEAGLE
B. Second keel absent; teeth without auxiliary points at base. Go to couplet 16.

16

A. Edges of teeth smooth
=MAKO
B. Edges of teeth serrated (saw toothed)
=WHITE SHARK

17

A. Base of first dorsal fin at least 4 times the height of fin
=FALSE CAT SHARK
B. Base of first dorsal fin much less than 4 times the height of the fin. Go to couplet 18.

18

A. Origin of first dorsal fin over or behind origin of pelvic fins. *Go to couplet 19.*

B. Origin of first dorsal fin well in front of origin of pelvic fins. *Go to couplet 21.*

19

A. Origin of first dorsal fin over origin of pelvic fins; a long barbel on each nostril =NURSE SHARK

B. Origin of first dorsal fin well behind origin of pelvic fins; barbels absent. *Go to couplet 20.*

20

A. Irregular chainlike markings on side of body =CHAIN DOGFISH

B. No chainlike markings on sides of body =DEEP-WATER CAT SHARK

21

A. Mouth at tip of snout =WHALE SHARK

B. Mouth not at tip of snout. *Go to couplet 22.*

22

A. First and second dorsal fins about equal in size. *Go to couplet 23.*

B. First dorsal fin much larger than second dorsal fin. *Go to couplet 25.*

23

A. All 5 gill openings in front of pectoral fins =SAND SHARK

B. Last 1 or 2 gill openings over or behind origin of pectoral fins. *Go to couplet 24.*

24

A. Origin of anal fin opposite CENTER of second dorsal fin; teeth
flat, blunt (pavement-like)   =SMOOTH DOGFISH
B. Origin of anal fin opposite ORIGIN of second dorsal fin; teeth
pointed and sharp   =LEMON SHARK

25

A. Origin of second dorsal fin about opposite CENTER of anal fin
=ATLANTIC SHARPNOSE SHARK
B. Origin of second dorsal fin about opposite the ORIGIN of anal
fin. *Go to couplet 26.*

26

A. Maximum length of pectoral fin as great as or greater than
distance from tip of snout to last gill opening; fins often
white at tips   =WHITETIP SHARK
B. Maximum length of pectoral fin less than distance from tip
of snout to last gill opening; fins without white tips. *Go to
couplet 27.*

27

A. Edges on both upper and lower teeth smooth
=FINETOOTH SHARK
B. Edges of upper teeth finely to strongly serrated; lower teeth
smooth or serrated. *Go to couplet 28.*

28

A. A low but distinct mid-dorsal ridge present in the skin between
first and second dorsal fins. *Go to couplet 29.*
B. Mid-dorsal ridge absent. *Go to couplet 32.*

29

A. Length of free rear tip of second dorsal fin more than twice as long as vertical height of the fin   =Sᴉᴄᴋʟᴇ Sʜᴀʀᴋ
B. Length of free rear tip of second dorsal fin less than twice as long as vertical height of the fin. *Go to couplet 30.*

30

A. Origin of first dorsal fin behind free inner angle of pectoral fin   =Dᴜsᴋʏ Sʜᴀʀᴋ
B. Origin of first dorsal fin over or forward of free inner angle of pectoral fin. *Go to couplet 31.*

31

A. Distance from front of mouth to tip of snout less than width of mouth   =Sᴀɴᴅʙᴀʀ Sʜᴀʀᴋ
B. Distance from front of mouth to tip of snout about equal to width of mouth   =Bɪɢɴᴏsᴇ Sʜᴀʀᴋ

32

A. Distance between nostrils greater than distance from front of mouth to tip of snout   =Bᴜʟʟ Sʜᴀʀᴋ
B. Distance between nostrils less than distance from front of mouth to tip of snout. *Go to couplet 33.*

33

A. Vertical height of first dorsal fin much greater than distance between tip of snout and eye; first gill opening less than 2½ times as long as horizontal diameter of eye; edges of lower teeth finely serrated   =Bʟᴀᴄᴋᴛɪᴘ Sʜᴀʀᴋ
B. Vertical height of first dorsal fin about equal to distance between tip of snout and eye; first gill opening more than 4 times as long as horizontal diameter of eye; edges of lower teeth smooth   =Sᴘɪɴɴᴇʀ Sʜᴀʀᴋ

APPENDIX II

U.S. NAVY "SHARK DANGER" RATINGS
(From General Principles of Diving: Marine Life—Sharks.)

Name	Danger*	Max. Size	Appearance†	Behavior	Where Found
White shark	4+	30 ft.	Slaty brown to black on back	Savage, aggressive	Oceanic; tropical, subtropical, warm temperate belts, especially in Australian waters
Mako shark	4+	30 ft.	Slender form; deep blue-gray on back	Savage	Oceanic, tropical, and warm temperate belts
Porbeagle shark	2+	12 ft.	Dark bluish gray on back	Sluggish except when pursuing prey	Continental waters of northern Atlantic. Allied forms in north Pacific, Australia, and New Zealand
Tiger shark	2+	30 ft.	Short snout, sharply pointed tail	Can be vigorous and powerful	Tropical and subtropical belts of all oceans, inshore and offshore
Lemon shark	2+	11 ft.	Yellowish brown on back; broadly rounded snout	Found in salt water creeks, bays, and sounds	Inshore western Atlantic, northern Brazil to North Carolina, tropical West Africa
Lake Nicaragua shark	2+	10 ft.	Dark gray on back	Found in shallow water	Fresh water species of Lake Nicaragua
Dusky shark	1+	14 ft.	Bluish or leaden gray on back	Found in shallow water	Tropical and warm temperate waters on both sides of Atlantic
White-Tipped shark	3+	13 ft.	Light gray to slaty blue on back	Indifferent, fearless	Tropical and subtropical Atlantic and Mediterranean. Deep offshore waters
Sand shark	2+	10 ft.	Bright gray-brown on back	Stays close to bottom	Indo-Pacific Mediterranean, tropical West Africa, South Africa, Gulf of Maine to Florida, Brazil, Argentina
Gray Nurse shark	3+	10 ft.	Pale gray on back	Swift and savage	Australia
Ganges River shark	4+	7 ft.	Gray on back	Ferocious, attacks bathers	Indian Ocean to Japan; ascends fresh water rivers
Hammerhead shark	4+	15 ft.	Ashy-gray on back; flat, wide head	Powerful swimmer	Warm temperate zone of all oceans including Mediterranean Sea, out at sea or close inshore

*1+ means minimum danger, 4+ means maximum danger.
†All sharks listed are of some shade of white on the under side.

APPENDIX III

Maximum sizes of common species of sharks

Species		Maximum length measured: U.S. coasts	Maximum length recorded: world	Traditional maximum size from literature
Common name	Scientific name			
Sixgill shark	*Hexanchus* sp.	15 feet 5 inches	––	26 feet 5 inches
Sand shark	*Carcharias taurus*	10 feet 5 inches	12 feet 3 inches	15 ft. 11 inches
Porbeagle	*Lamna nasus*	10 feet	12 feet	12 feet
Salmon shark	*Lamna ditropis*	8 feet 6 inches	8 feet 6 inches	12 feet
Mako	*Isurus oxyrinchus*	10 feet 6 inches	12 feet	12 feet-13 feet
White shark	*Carcharodon carcharias*	18 feet 2 inches	21 feet	36 feet 6 inches
Basking shark	*Cetorhinus maximus*	32 feet 2 inches	45 feet	40 feet-50 feet
Thresher shark	*Alopias vulpinus*	18 feet	18 feet	20 feet
Nurse shark	*Ginglymostoma cirratum*	9 feet 3 inches	––	14 feet
Whale shark	*Rhincodon typus*	38 feet	45 feet	45 feet-50 feet
Chain dogfish	*Scyliorhinus retifer*	1 foot 5 inches	––	2 feet 6 inches
Leopard shark	*Triakis semifasciata*	5 feet	––	5 feet
Smooth dogfish	*Mustelus canis*	4 feet 9 inches	––	5 feet
Tiger shark	*Galeocerdo cuvieri*	13 ft. 10 inches	18 feet	30 feet
Soupfin shark	*Galeorhinus zyopterus*	6 feet 5 inches	6 feet 5 inches	6 feet 5 inches
Blue shark	*Prionace glauca*	11 feet	12 feet 7 inches	25 feet
Bull shark	*Carcharhinus leucas*	9 feet 10 inches	––	10 feet
Whitetip shark	*Carcharhinus longimanus*	11 feet 6 inches	––	12 feet
Sandbar shark	*Carcharhinus milberti*	7 feet 8 inches	––	8 feet
Dusky shark	*Carcharhinus obscurus*	11 ft. 11 inches	––	15 feet
Bonnethead	*Sphyrna tiburo*	3 feet 7 inches	––	6 feet
Great hammerhead	*Sphyrna mokarran*	18 feet 4 inches	––	15 feet
Spiny dogfish	*Squalus acanthias*	5 feet 3 inches	––	5 feet
Green dogfish	*Etmopterus virens*	0 feet 11 inches	––	––
Midwater dogfish	*Squaliolus* sp.	0 feet 7 inches	––	––
Greenland shark	*Somniosus microcephalus*	16 feet 6 inches	21 feet	24 feet
Sawshark	*Pristiophorus schroederi*	2 feet 10 inches	––	––
Angel shark	*Squatina dumeril*	4 feet 5 inches	––	––

BIBLIOGRAPHY

Baldridge, Jr., Captain D. H., USN, and Williams, J. "Shark Attack: Feeding or Fighting?" *Military Medicine.* February 1969.

Brossard, C. and Karales, J. H. "The Lady and the Sharks." *Look.* July 12, 1966.

Casey, J. G. *Angler's Guide to Sharks of the Northeastern United States.* U. S. Department of the Interior, Bureau of Sport Fisheries and Wildlife, Cir. No. 179. Washington, D.C., April 1964.

———*Abstracts of Current Investigations in the United States Dealing with the Elasmobranch Fishes.* American Institute of Biological Sciences. Washington, D.C., 1967–1968.

———*Conference on the Shark-Porpoise Relationship.* The American Institute of Biological Sciences. Washington, D.C., 1967.

Coppleson, V. M. *Shark Attack!* Angus & Robertson. Sydney, Australia, 1962.

Fox, R. "Attacked by a Killer Shark!" *Readers' Digest.* August 1965.

Gilbert, P. W., Schultz, L. P. and Springer, S. "Shark Attacks During 1959." *Science.* Vol. 132, No. 3423, August 5, 1960.

———*Sharks and Survival.* D. C. Heath and Co. Boston, 1963.

———"Some Facts About Sharks." *The New York Times Magazine.* August 5, 1962.

———"The Shark: Barbarian and Benefactor." *BioScience.* Vol. 18, No. 10, October 1968.

Hartley, William and Ellen. "SHARK! Overrated Demon or General Scourge?" *Science Digest.* June 1967.

Helm, T. *Shark! Unpredictable Killer of the Sea.* Dodd, Mead & Co. New York, 1961.

Herre, A. W. C. T. "Sharks in Fresh Water." *Science.* 122:417, September 2, 1955.

———"Sharks Attracted by Low Pulsing Sounds." *Science News Letter.* 84:345, November 30, 1963.

———"Shark Finds Food Fast by Underwater Sounds." *Science News Letter.* 86:200, September 26, 1964.

Kato, S., Springer, S. and Wagner, M. H. *Field Guide to Eastern Pacific and Hawaiian Sharks.* U. S. Department of Interior, Fish and Wildlife Service, Cir. 271. Washington, D.C., December 1967.

———*The 1960, and the 1965 Salt-Water Angling Survey.* U. S. Department of the Interior, Fish & Wildlife Service, Cir. 153 and Research Pub. 67. Washington, D.C.

———*Progress in Sport Fishery Research 1967.* Bureau of Sport Fisheries and Wildlife, Resource Pub. 64. Washington, D.C., May 1968.

Llano, G. A. "Sharks Vs. Men." *Scientific American.* 1966:54–61, June, 1957.

McClane, A. J. *McClane's Standard Fishing Encyclopedia and International Angling Guide.* Holt, Rinehart and Winston. New York, 1965.

McCormick, H. W. and Allen, T. with Captain Young, W. E. *Shadows in the Sea.* Chilton Co., Philadelphia, 1963.

———"Marvels and Mysteries of Our Animal World." *Readers' Digest.* 1964.

Kenny, N. T. "Sharks: Wolves of the Sea." *National Geographic.* February 1968.

Nelson, D. R. and Gruber, S. H. "Sharks: Attraction by Low-frequency Sounds." *Science.* 142:975, November 1963.

Ommanney, F. D. and the editors of *Life. The Fishes.* Time, Inc., New York, 1962.

Phinizy, C. "The Sharks Are Moving In." *Sports Illustrated.* 29:68–72, December 9, 1968.

Rhodes, F. H. T., Zim, H. S. and Shaffer, P. R. *Fossils. A Guide to Prehistoric Life.* Golden Press. New York, 1962.

Sand, G. X. "He Stalks Sharks by Kayak." *Popular Mechanics.* May 1966.

Scott, J. D. "Daredevil Sport: Shark Tagging." *Sports Afield.* March 1965.

Stephens, W. M. "The Lady and the Sharks." *Saturday Evening Post.* July 4, 1959.

Thompson, J. R. and Springer, S. *Sharks, Skates, Rays and Chimaeras.* U. S. Department of the Interior, Fish and Wildlife Service, Cir. 228. Washington, D.C., September 1965.

Young, W. E. with Mazet, H. S. *Shark! Shark! the Thirty-Year Odyssey of a Pioneer Shark Hunter.* Gotham House. New York, 1934.

———"Current Investigations at the Mote Marine Laboratory." Research abstracts. Sarasota, Florida, January–December, 1968.

INDEX

Abalones, 25, 26
Adamson, Dr. Richard H., 139
Africa, 14, 15, 139. *See* South *and* West
Age. *See* Growth rings
Age of Fishes, 35
AIBS. *See* American Institute of Biological Sciences
Alabama, 37
Alps, 35
American Institute of Biological Sciences (AIBS), 126. *See also* Shark Research Panel
American Museum of Natural History, 37, 112
Anatomy, 41–55, 113–14, 132; bite, 47; body covering, 47; brain, 47, 49; "breathing" apparatus, 44–45; color detection, 50–51; digestive system, 51–53; eyes, 49–50, 133; food storage, 52; jaws, 47; lateralis system, 130; liver, 45, 51, 53, 140; pups, 43; reproduction methods, 42–43; sensory system, 49, 132; "skin teeth," 47; stomach, 52–54; "swimming" relationship, 44–45; teeth, 46, 133–34; weight, 45
Ancestry, 14, 35–40; *Cladoselache,* 35–36; Devonian Period, 35; early forms, 35, 37; fossil evidence, 35–36; hybodonts, 36; modern, 36; prehistoric, 36; relics, 36, 38; survival ability, 39
Andes, 35
"Anglers' Guide to Sharks," 89
Apalachicola River, 37
Aquariums, 54, 112, 116
Aristotle, 16
Asia, 139
Atlantic Ocean, 59, 60, 61, 64, 66, 69, 75
Attacks (on man), 23, 24–29, 78–79, 98, 127, 129, 135; abrasion wounds, 47, *ill.* 48; area, 34; causes, 45, 132 (*see* theories); deliberateness, controversy, 23, 29, 30; discouraging, 84–86; divers, 134; documented record (1959), 33–34; incidence, 134; inducements to, 34; mistaken identity, 29, 30; patterns of similarity, 80–81; pictorial record, 15; positions, 47; possibility of, 41, 86, 118; records, 41; repellents, 81–84, 126 (*see* Science); theories, 79–80, 129; threat of, 138; time of,

78; U.S., 34; water temperature, 81; worldwide timetable, 81. *See also* Color perception *and* Survivors
Australia, 52, 54, 56, 59, 60, 61, 64, 71, 72, 75, 76, 81, 88, 91, 109–10, 116; attacks, 34, 47, 76, 78–79; food, 139; "meshing," 81; Museum, 78; nets, 44
Authorities, 33, 80, 98, 111, 121

Bahamas, 47, 66, 127. *See* Bimini
Bait, for shark fishing, 93, 108, 109, *ill.* 90; launching, 99–104, 106, *ill.* 103
Baja California, 66
Baker's Beach, 24
Bakersfield, California, 37
Baldridge, Capt. David H., 7, 53, 98, 126, 129, 138
Balloons, 102–4
Bane, Gilbert W., 134
Barbados, 60, 137
Barnacle Lil, 109–10
Barnes, Majorie, 8
Barracuda, 23, 97
Bartow, Florida, 38
Basking shark, 43, 74–75; *ill.* 48
Bay shark, 60
Bay Shore, L.I., New York, 89
Beach Haven, New Jersey, 79
Beaches, protecting, 81–82, 127
Behavior, experiments, 114–16, 135
Benefactors, 137, 138–41
Bible, 15–16
Big-game fishing, 90, 100, 105, 106
Bimini, 47, 84, 123, 127, 128, 133. *See* Lerner Marine Laboratory
Biologists, 7, 33, 43, 83, 122, 135, 136
Biochemists, 7, 53
Birds, 50
Bite-meter, 133
Black-tip shark, 14; fishing or, 91; as food, 140; large, 67–68; small, 66–67
Black whaler, 61
Blood, effect on shark, 47, 82, 83, 84
Blue pointer shark, 59, 61, 78, 87. *See* Great blue shark *and* Mako shark

Blue shark, 61, 69, 70, 91, 134; as food, 140; migrations, 137. *See* Great blue shark *and* Porbeagle
Blue whaler, 14, 61. *See* Great blue shark
Bodega Bay, California, 26
Bone shark, 74. *See* Basking shark
Bonito, 93, 99–100, 103, 134
Bonnethead shark, 62, 63
Borden Milk Company, 140
Bottom-dwelling species, 44–45
Boynton Beach Inlet, Florida, 99, 100, 102, 105, 106
Brady, Patrick, 55
Brazil, 59, 64, 66, 69
Brontosaurus, 36
Bronze whaler, 60, 61. *See also* Bay shark
Brown shark, *ill.* 48, 117
Brown whaler, 61
Bruder, Charles, 79
Bubble curtain, 127
Bull shark, 40, 65–66, 91, 106; as food, 140
Buoyancy, 45, 49, 53

Caladesi Island, 120
California, 36–37, 75, 134; attacks, 24–26
California State College (Long Beach), 134
Cancer, 139
Cape Hatteras, 66
Cape Haze Marine Laboratory, 111, 113, 116, 118, 126–27. *See* Mote Marine Laboratory
Cape Kennedy, 107
Carcharodon, 37; *ill.* 38
Carconetta, 66. *See* Black-tip shark
Caribbean, 40, 64, 65, 66, 72, 141
Carter, Howard, 135
Casey, John G., 7, 136–37
Cat shark, *ill.* 48
Central America, 39–40, 64, 137, 139
Chain dogfish, 43
Chesapeake Bay, 37, 137
China, 66, 75
Chipola River, 36, 37
Chum (bait), 93; *ill.* 90
Clark, Dr. Eugenie, 111–18, 126–27; *ill.* 113
Clearwater, Florida, 108
Clem, Dr. L. William, 139
Cleveland Shales, 36
Clubs, shark fishing, 88–89, 97
Coastal sharks, 45
Color perception, 50–51, 116, 127, 133. *See under* species
Coogee Aquarium, 54
Coppleson, Dr. V. M., 79–81
Cornell University, 33, 132, 133, 139
Cousteau, Jacques-Yves, 42
Creasey, Roger, 134
Crime, 54–55
Cuba, 141
Cub shark, 40, 65. *See* Bull shark

Daiber, Franklin, 139
Dailey, Murray D., 134
Dean, Alfred, 91, 109–10
Descades, 14
De Sylva, Dr. Donald, 98
Devi River, 71
Devonian Period, 39
Diet. *See under* species
Dinosaur, 36, 39
Divers, 14, 17, 34, 42, 134; danger zone, 34. *See* skindivers
Diving, 42, 76; vanes, 62

Dogfish shark, 36
Dolphins, 37, 52, 119
Dolphin Skindiving Club, 27, 29, 31
Dow Chemical Corporation, 139
Durban, South Africa, 81–82, 87
Dusky sharks, 123, 133
Dynamometer, 91

Eastman, Paul, 80
Ecuador, 64, 75
Ego, Kenji, 136
Egyptians, 15
Elephant shark, 74. *See* Basking shark
England, 88, 139
Europe, 139
Experimental use of sharks, 138–41
Exploration, of the sea, 42

Families, number of, 56
Farming, ocean floor, 42
Fatalities, from attacks, 34
Fear, of shark, 41–42
Feeding, 47; coastal waters, 90; frenzy, 47, 58, 68, 83; nighttime, 50; time, 78; vision, relationship, 128
Fighting the shark, 76–86
Fish, 119; as bait, 93; cold-blooded, 51; growth rings, 116; largest in world, 72; oil, effect on shark, 47; predator, 39; shark as food, 139–40
Fishing, *ill.* 21; big-game, 90, 100, 105, 106; commercial mackerel, 97–98; kayak, 106–8; longline, 135–36; shark populations, relationship, 135–36; winching, 87. *See* Shark fishing
"Fish 'n' chips," 139
Fleet, Verne, S., 26
Florida, 58, 64, 66, 69, 71, 72, 73, 88, 133, 137; Board of Conservation Marine Laboratory, 97; commercial fisheries, 97–98; fossil shark teeth, 36, 37; geological sites, 37; Gulf Coast, 27, 112–13; Keys, 92; sharks, 26 ff., 88–89, 98; tourism, 96–98
Florida Shark Club (Jacksonville), 8, 80, 89, 107
Food, shark as, 139–40
Fort Lauderdale, Florida, 97
Fort Rucker, Alabama, 30
Fossils, 37, 38
Fox, Rodney, 76–78
Francis, A. V., 33
Fresh-water sharks, 39–40
Frilled sharks, 36
Fryling, Duffie, 26
Fudge, Bob, *ill.* 107

Gaff hook, 105; *ill.* 106
Galler, Dr. Sidney R., 33, 83
Gama, Vasco da, 14
Ganges River, 71; shark, 40, 70–71
Geologists, 36
George's River, 79
Gilbert, Dr. Perry W., 7, 33, 83, 84, 98, 118, 119, 123, 124, 127–28, 133, 139; *ill.* 117
Gladiatorial events, 20, 22
Gnathodynamometer (bite-meter), 133
Goodman, Herb, 8, 89, 99–105; *ill.* 101
Gray nurse shark, 71, 78
Great Australian Bight, 109–10
Great blue shark, 61–62
Great white (*or* Man-eater) shark, 14, 25, 26, 56–57, 134, *ill.* 16, 46, 113; ancestor, 37, 38; attack, 76–78; big-game fish, 90–91; *ill.* 91;

catching, 87, 109; pull, 92; record size catch, 110; weight, 109
Greeks, 15–17
Groom, Ronnie, 27
Ground shark, 65. *See* Bull shark
Grover, Danny, 27–29
Grover, Ernest, 27–30
Growth rings, 116, 136
Gruber, Samuel, 132–33
Guinan, John A., 8
Guitarfish, 42
Gulf Coast (Florida), 27, 112–13
Gulf of Arabia, 64
Gulf of Maine, 69, 70, 74, 75
Gulf of Mexico, 37, 60, 64, 66, 120, 122

Hammerhead shark, 14, 33, 62–64, 78, 102, 134, *ill.* 27, 101; attack, 26; catching, 104–5; porpoise attack, 120–21; pull, 91–92; repellent, 84; species, 62
Harmless sharks, 72–75
Harvard University, 130
Hawaii, 58, 64, 135; control and research program, 136; legends, 17–20, 22. *See* University
Hay, James, 26
Hearing, sense of, 49, 128, 129–30; experiments, 130–32; human ranges, 131
Hebrews, 15
Heller, Dr. John H., 116
Helm, Thomas, 120
Herodotus, 16
Hicks, John, 84
Himalayas, 35
Hobson, Albert, 54
Holms, Reginald W., 55
Holt, Deane, 33
Hopkins, Sir John, 15
Hunter College, 112
Hunting sharks, 108–9
Hybodonts, 36
Hydrophone, 130

Ice Age, 38
Iceland, 75
Ichthyology, 30, 112
Idaho, 37
IGFA. *See* International Game Fish Association
India, 15, 40, 64, 66, 71
Indian Ocean, 71, 109
Indians, 37
Indo-China, 64
Indo-Pacific, 59
Industry, 141
Institute of Marine Science (Miami), 30, 98
Institute of Neurological Diseases and Blindness, 139
Institutions, research, 132
Intercoastal Waterway, 102
International Game Fish Association, 90, 94
Ireland, 75
Ischia (Lacco Ameno), 15

Jacksonville, Florida, 80, 88, 89, 97
Japan, 71, 75, 139
Jewelry, from fossil teeth, 38
Johnson, Dr. C. Scott, 45, 84; *ill.* 85
Jonah, 15–16
Jurassic Period, 36

Kain-alu Grove, 20
Kalei, 17–18
Kamo-hoa-lii (shark god), 17–20

Kansas, 37
Kayaks, 106–8
Greeks, 15
Kētos, 15
Key West, Florida, 53, 108
Killers, *ill.* 16. *See* Man-eating sharks
Kimmel, George, 29
Klopfer, Dr. Dudley, 134
Kogler, Albert, 24–25, 27, 81

Lady with a Spear, 112
La Jolla, California, 26, 112, 127, 133; Cove, 25
Lake Nicaragua, 65, 137; shark, 39–40, 65
Lake Worth, Florida, 89, 99, 100
Land shark, 97
Larson, Lee, 31
Leather, 141
Legends and myths, 17, 20, 22
Lehrer, Gerald, 25–26
Lemon shark, 64, 91, 106, 111, 123, 124, 128, 133, *ill.* 50; experiments, 114–15; as food, 140; repellent, 84
Leonidas of Terentum, 17
Leopard shark. *See* Tiger shark
Lerner Marine Laboratory, 47, 83, 123, 127, 133, 139. *See* Bimini
Link, Edwin A., 42
Linnaeus, 16
Litters, 43
"Living fossils," 38
Logan, Ben, 106–8
London, England, 15
Long Island, 60, 69, 73, 89
Louisiana, 65

McClure, Don, 97
McKee, James, 26–27
Mackerel shark, 69. *See* Porbeagle
McKiver, Sonny, 27, 28
Maine, 59, 89, 137, 138. *See also* Gulf
Mako shark, 14, 31, 58–59, 69; big-game fish, 90, 91; as food, 140. *See* Porbeagle
Malibu, California, 26
Mammals, 16, 119
Mammoths, 39
Man, origin, 35
Man-eating sharks, 25, 40. 56–75, *ill.* 46; bay, 60; black-tip, 66–68; bull, 65–66; Ganges, 70–71; great blue, 61–62; great white, 56–57; hammerhead, 62–64; lemon, 64; mackerel (*see* porbeagle); mako, 58–59; most-feared, 76 (*see* great white); nurse, 71–72; porbeagle, 69–70; sand, 68–69; tiger, 57–58; whaler, 61; white-tipped, 59–60. *See* Great white shark *and under* species
Manta ray, 107, 118
Marathon, Florida, 26–27
Marineland, Florida, 8; Research Laboratory, 121
Marlin, 47, 105
Martha's Vineyard, 137
Maryland, 37
Massachusetts, 57, 74
Matawan Creek, New Jersey, 79
Mathewson, Robert F., 123, 124
Maui, 19
Medical research, 116–17, 138–41
Mediterranean, 69
Meshing, 81–82
Mexico, 34, 60, 139, 141
Miami, Florida, 71, 88; Institute of Marine Science, 98
Miocene Period, 36

Mississippi River, 40
Modern sharks, beginning, 36
Mohoalii (god), 20
Molokai, 19; Shark Hill, 20
Montauk, Long Island, 88, 91
Monterey Bay, California, 88
Moss Landing, California, 88
Mote Marine Laboratory, 7, 45, 51, 53, 91, 118, 126, 129, 133, 134, 139; director, 118; ill. 135
Mote Scientific Foundation, 118
Mountain ranges, 35
Mount Desert Laboratory, 138
Mundus, Frank, 91
Murder, 54–55
Myrberg, Dr. Arthur A., 131
Myths, 22–23, 75

National Cancer Institute, 139
National Heart Institute, 139
National Institute of Mental Health, 139
National Institutes of Health, 138
Naturalists, 16
Naval Ship Research and Development Laboratory, 8
Neal, Lt. James C., 30–32
Nelson, Donald R., 130, 135
Nets, 44
Newark, New Jersey, 141
New England, 66; Institute for Medical Research, 116
New Jersey, 37, 58, 64, 74, 79–80, 89, 127
New Mexico, 37
New Orleans, 126
New York, 37, 66, 74; Aquarium, 112
New York University, 112
New Zealand, 59, 61
Nicaragua, 40
Nickname, 47
North Carolina, 63, 64, 70, 72, 89, 137
North Sea, 70
Norway, 75
Nurse sharks, 44, 71–72, 111, 133; fishing for, 91; as food, 140

Oahu, Hawaii, 135, 136
Oceanarium, 121
Ocean City Leather Company, 141
Oceanic Institute (Hawaii), 136
Oil (shark), 75, 140
Olive, Dr. John R., 33
O'Neill, Shirley, 24–25

Pacific Ocean, 15, 60, 61, 66, 75
Pacific Railway Survey, 36
Palau Islands, 112
Paleontologists, 35–36, 37
Palm Beach, Florida, 98, 129
Palm Beach Sharkers, 89, 97
Pamparin, Robert L., 25–26, 127
Panama City, Florida, 8, 27–29, 30–32; News-Herald, 29
Parasites, 134
Parker, Dr. George H., 130, 132
Parmian Period, 36
Pearl divers, 14
Pearl Harbor, shark pen, 20, 22
Pebble phosphate pits, 38
Pelagic species, 45, 75
Pens, 20, 22, 113, 114, 123; ill. 135
Pensacola, Florida, 54
Persian fleet, 16
Peru, 66, 75

Philippines, 112
Pigafetta, Antonio, 14
Pitts, Bradley, 27
Placida, Florida, 111
Planey, Andrew H., 8
Plankton, 73, 74
Pliny, 17
Plouff, James, 32–33
Plutarch, 119
Plymouth, 133
Population (shark), 135–36; control, 140–41
Porbeagle shark, 69–70, 91
Porpoises, 37, 42, 119–25; characteristics, 119–20; shark, relationship, 120–25; species, 119
Port Everglades, Florida, 32
Port Jackson shark, 36
"Powerhead," 108–9
Prehistoric shark, 36
Pteranodons, 39
Pull, of sharks, 91–92
Pups, 43, 116
Puumano (Shark Hill), 20

Ralls, Dr. David P., 139
Range. See under species
Rays (fish), 42
Records: 1916, 79–80
Redman, David W., 8
Redmon, Bill, Jr., 30
Red Sea, 66, 112
Relics, 36
Remoras, 40
Repellents, 126, 127–28, 129, 138
Reptiles, 39, 50
Requiem masses, 56
Requiem shark, 56, 65, 66. See Bull shark
Research, 51, 83, 84, 111, 112, 113–15, 123–25; census, 134; conferences, 126; control program, 135–36; costs, 125; government, 126; grants, 132; medical, 116–17, 138–41; new, 132; programs, 34, international, 126; number, 132; tools, 130, 133. See Science
Rhode Island, 72
Rivas, Luis R., 30
River sharks, 40
Riviera Beach, Florida, 98
Robins, Dr. C. Richard, 30
Rockies, 35
Rogers, Paul, 98
"Rogue shark," theory, 79, 80

Safety rules, 84–86
Sailfish, 105
Sailfish shark, 74. See Basking shark
St. Augustine, Florida, 80, 121
St. Petersburg, Florida, 97
Salerno, Florida, 140
Samples, Steven, 98, 129
Sandbanks, 81
Sandbar sharks, 137
San Diego, California, 25, 84; Bay, 60
San Francisco Bay, 24, 81
Sand (or sand tiger) shark, 43, 68–69, 71; ill. 44, 48
Sandy Hook Marine Laboratory, 89
San Juan River, 40, 137
Sarasota, Florida, 7, 45, 126, 134; ill. 135
Saults, Dan, 8
Sawfish, 40, 42
Scalloped hammerhead shark, 62
Scallops, 120
Scent, sharks and, 47, 49

INDEX

School shark, 139
Schultz, Dr. Leonard P., 33, 126
Schurke, 15
Science, 126–37
Scotland, 75
Scott, Hugh H., 7
Scott, Roberta, 7
Scripps Institute of Oceanography, 112, 113, 133
Scuba divers, 134
Sea, the, 42, 81, 112
Sea cows, 37
SEALAB, 125
Sebastian Inlet, Florida, 106, 107
Sea lions, 37
Seals, 37, 109
Sea-serpent stories, 75
Selachians, 42
Seymour, Gary, 31
Shadows in the Sea, 52, 71
Sharkathon, 27, 89
Shark Attack!, 79
Shark Attack Files, 80, 126
Shark Chaser, 83, 126, 128, 138
Shark fever, 88
Shark fishing, 87–98; bait, 93, 108, 109, *ill.* 90, launching, 99–100, 101, 102–4, 106, *ill.* 103; big-game species, 90–91; catch, 106, 110, per year, 89; record, 110, weighing, 94–95; chum (bait), 93, *ill.* 90; clubs, 88–89, 97; commercial, 17, 98, 140–41; dangers, 94; dynamometer, 91; encouraging, 98; equipment, 93, 110; "fever," 88; fighting category, 90–91; gaff hook, 105, *ill.* 106; hunting, 108–9; jaws, as trophies, 95, *ill.* 97; from kayak, 106–8; locating, 93; participants, 88; popularity, 96; population control, 135–36; "powerhead," 108–9; problems, 105; prohibitions, 97; pull, 91–92; from shore, 93; skindiving, 114; "snapper line," 94; specialists, 99–110; tackle, 92–93; tagging program, 89, technique, 93–94; tourism, 96–98
Shark gods, 20
Shark Hill, 20
Shark-men (legend), 18–20
Shark priest, 19, 20
Shark Research Panel (SRP), 7, 33, 83, 84, 98, 119, 126, 129
Sharks: adaptability, 39–40; aliases, 69; anatomy (*see* Anatomy); ancestry (*see* Ancestry); bait for, 93, 99–104, 106, 108, 109 (*see also* Chum); behavior, 114–16, 135; as benefactors, 137, 138–41; blood, 47, 82, 83, 84; buoyancy, 45, 49, 53; cannibalism, intrauterine, 43; in captivity, 51, 52, 113, 114, 116; census-taking, 134; characteristics, 14–15, 16, 17, 22, 35–36, 39–40, 45–46, 84–85, 113, 118, 129, 134–35 (*see also under* species); classification, 42, 56; collecting, 113–14; conditioning, 116; controlling, 111; courtship, 129; danger, 42, 98, 141; death, 51, 94; eating habits, 51, 114, 117, 118 (*see* Feeding); enemies, 119 (*see* Porpoises); eyesight, 49–50, 128, 132–33 (*see also* Color perception); as food, 139–40; identification, 142–48; intelligence, 134–35; jaws, 133; legends and myths, 17, 20, 22; mating, 66; migration, 134, 136, 137; names, 14; -offspring relationship, 43–44; pain, 51; pull, 91–92; reproduction, 116; sleep, 116; smell, sense of, 47, 49, 84, 128–29, 130, 132; species, 42, 56, 65; teeth (*see* Teeth); weight, 45, 94–95; word, derivation, 15; worship of, 20. *See also*

Attacks, Man-eating, *and under* name of species
Shark screen, 84, 127, *ill.* 85
Shark! Shark!, 17
Shark-tagging program, 89
Sharktooth Hill, 37
Shark! Unpredictable Killer of the Sea, 120
"Shark year," 80
Sharp-nosed mackerel shark. *See* Mako shark
Sharp-nose sharks, 40
Sheldon, Ralph E., 128
Shellfish diving, 34
Sherman, Jeff, 31
Shovelhead shark, 62
Shows, Bill, *ill.* 90
Shows, Bing, 89
Shrimpboats, 67
Siakong, 112
Sierra Leones, 14
Sigel, Dr. Michael, 139
Silky shark, 91, 92
Silurian Period, 35
Skeleton (of sharks), 42
Skindivers (ing), 26, 30, 71, 76, 108, 112, 127, 130; advice, 118; attacks on, 134; contests, 76; for sharks, 114; Siakong, 112
"Skin teeth," 47, *ill.* 48
Slaughter, Scotty, 108–9
Small, Dr. Parker A., 139
Smith, James, 55
Smithsonian Institution, 33, 134
Smooth dogfish, *ill.* 48
Smooth hammerhead shark, 62
Snodgrass, James, 133
Sound, -shark, relationship, 130
Soupfin shark, 140
South Africa, 40, 59, 69, 70, 81–82, 87, 88; shark nets, 44
South America, 34, 66, 139; attacks, 34
South Carolina, 37
South Pacific, 17
South Sea Islanders, 20
Spanish shark, 68. *See* Sand shark
Spearfishing, 34, 76–77, 84
Species, 42, 56, 65
Spinner shark, 66, 91. *See* Black-tip shark
Spiny dogfish, 138
Sponge divers, 17
Spot-fin shark, 66. *See* Black-tip shark
Springer, Stewart, 7, 33, 43, 91, 98, 122
Spring Lake, New Jersey, 79
Squalene, 116–17
Sting ray, 97, 100
Submarines, 62
Sullivan, Jim, 29
Sunfish, 74. *See* Basking shark
Superstitions, 62
"Survival sack," 84
Survivors (of sea disasters), 60, 61, 82–83, 127
Swan River whaler, 61
Swimming, 44–45, 50, 81; safety rules, 34, 84–86
Swordfish, 140
Sydney, Australia, 54–55, 78, 79, 81

Tagging programs, 136–37
Tarpon, 40, 106
Teeth, 22, 36–38, 46, 133–34
Tester, Dr. Albert L., 33, 127, 129, 136
Thermal zone, 81
Thorson, Thomas B., 137
Thresher shark, 14, 91; *ill.* 48

Tiger sharks, 14, 45, 54, 57–58, 78, 84, 91, 106, 123, 127, 133, 136; *ill.* 48, 52, 107, 124; stomach contents, 52–53; value, 141
Time, of attacks, 34
Tourism, 96–98
Tournaments, 89
Transducer, 130, 131
Trophies, 95, *ill.* 97
Tulane University, 126

UCLA Bone Research Laboratory, 139
Underwater Society of America, 98
UN Food and Agriculture Organization, 140
Universities, research programs, 132
University of California, 134
University of Delaware, 139
University of Hawaii, 33, 129, 132, 136
University of Maryland, 118
University of Miami, 30, 132; Institute of Marine Science, 130, 131
University of Nebraska, 137
U. S. Air Mine Development Unit, 31
U. S. Bureau of Commercial Fisheries, 8, 33, 98, 122
U. S. Coast Guard, 33; Search and Rescue Agency, 82
U. S. Department of Interior: Bureau of Sport Fisheries and Wildlife, 7–8, 137
U. S. Fish and Wildlife Service, 7, 89
U. S. Government Printing Office, 89
U. S. Navy, 7, 20, 83, 98, 138; Medical Institute, 139; Mine Defense Laboratory, 32; Office of Naval Research, 33, 112, 118, 126; Undersea Warfare Center, 84

Value, 141
Vanderbilt, Alfred, 112
Vanderbilt, William, 112
Van Sant, Charles, 79
Variety Children's Research Foundation, 139
Venice, Florida, 37
Vitamins, 140

Walker, Robert, 32–33
Washington State University, 134
Water temperature, for shark activity, 34
Weaver, Billy, 135
Weighing, formula for, 94–95
West Africa, 64, 69
Whaler shark, 61, 78
Whales, 15–16, 37, 119
Whale shark, 16, 36, 72–73
White death. *See* Great white shark
White pointer. *See* Great white shark
White shark, 16, 78. *See* Great white shark
White-tipped shark, 59–60, 122
Whitley, Gilbert P., 78
Wisby, Dr. Warren J., 130–31
Wood, F. G., 121
Woods Hole Marine Biological Laboratory, 128
World War II, 82, 83, 126, 140
Writings, on sharks, 16–17

Young, Capt. William E., 17, 52, 53, 71, 127

Zambezi River, 40

ROBERT F. BURGESS was born in Grand Rapids, Michigan, in 1927. There he acquired an early interest in outdoor adventure. As a boy he hunted and fished throughout northern Michigan and built diving gear to explore a shipwreck believed to be LaSalle's lost *Griffon*. Mr. Burgess joined the Army Ski Troops at the end of World War II and spent a year in the Italian Alps. He returned to Europe after his discharge to study in Italy and at the University of Neuchatel in Switzerland. He learned to spearfish while living on the Isle of Capri. He completed his education in journalism at Michigan State University and developed his first interest in sharks when he began sport fishing for them as a free-lance writer and photographer in Florida. Mr. Burgess' stories, articles and photographs have appeared in many magazines in this country and abroad.

Mr. Burgess is married and lives in Chattahoochee, Florida, where he is an avid fisherman and underwater photographer.

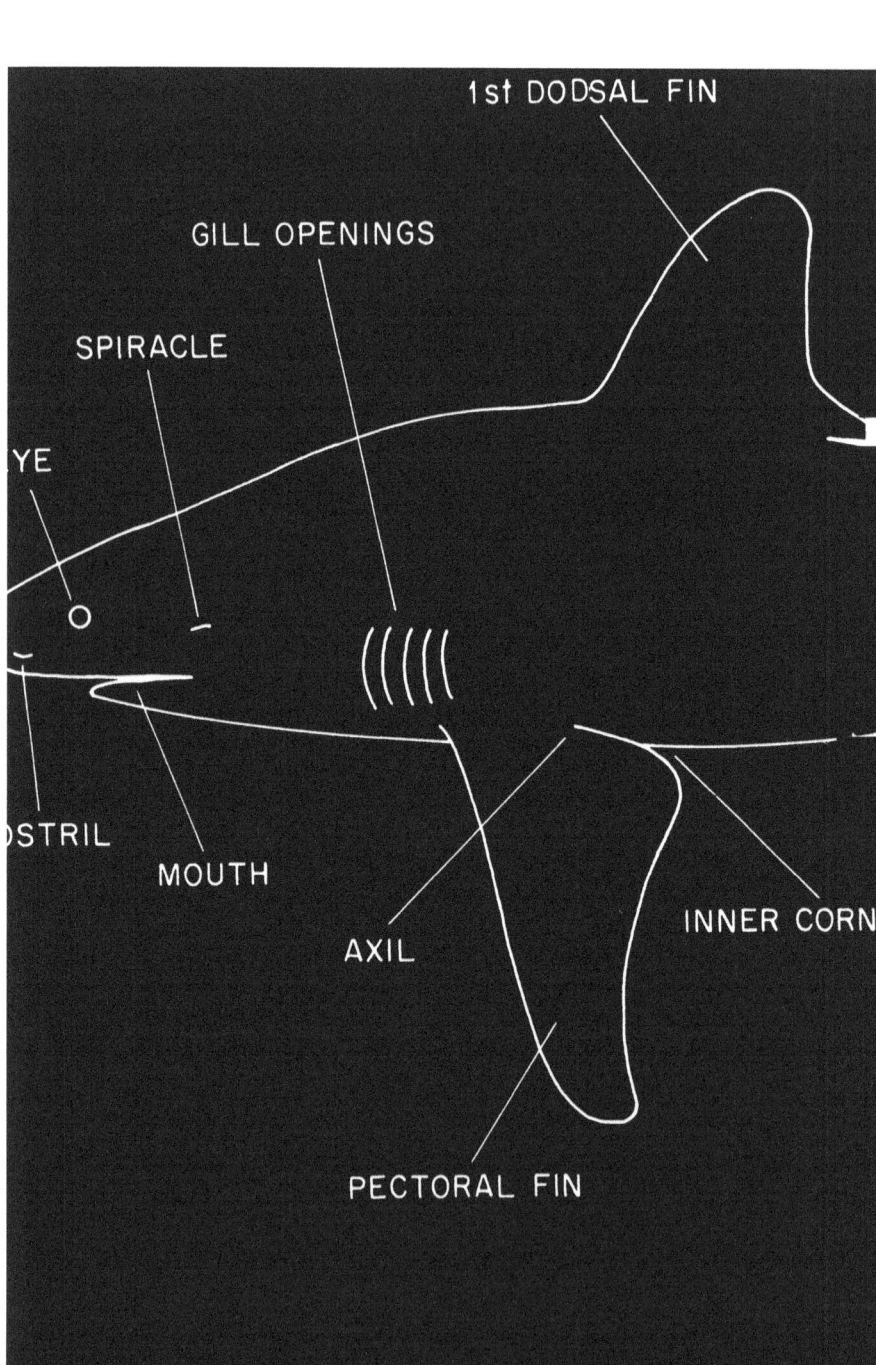